THE ROAD TO NOWHERE

How to be a successful failure in the music industry!

Tales and tips from a lifetime playing in
bands you've never heard of...

by
Johnny Samson

©2021 Riverflow Books, All Rights Reserved

CONTENTS

HELLO CLEVELAND — 5

Being in a band is damn cool, but why is that? And what do you actually do? And more to the point, why do you do it? And why does everybody keep asking when are you going to get a real job?

LEARNING TO PLAY — 11

Anyone can teach themselves to play an instrument and form a rock'n'roll band. It is dead easy. (Warning: do not underestimate the value of actually learning to do something properly. Which is dead hard.)

FORMING A BAND — 15

The first time it's great fun, as inevitably it's you and your best mates. After that, it gets exponentially more difficult and oh my word, some of the people you'll meet...

WRITING A SONG — 35

Note - contains no hints whatsoever on how to write a song. I can't help you there. But make sure when you do write one that you all agree on who wrote what when you wrote it rather than disagree on who wrote what many years after you wrote it.

THE REHEARSAL ROOM — 43

'Tis a well-known fact that rehearsal rooms are among the worst rooms in the world in terms of décor, scent, affordability and general ambiance. They rank just above a smack den, and just below rooms where they shoot cheap porn films.

BOOKING A GIG — 55

There is no experience in the world as rewarding and straight forward as booking gigs for a band. And the people you encounter are just the best people. Honestly.

THE MANAGER — 73

You want one, we all want one. But be very careful what you wish for. And never forget the cardinal rule – show me the money!

THE RECORD COMPANY — 81

To be honest, this chapter is singularly unhelpful, principally because the lack of success of all my bands over the years necessitates that, by definition, I had very little to do with record companies. You can probably skip this and go straight to the next one.

IN THE STUDIO — 85

There are very few things for a young band that seem as exciting as going into the studio to record your masterpiece. And very few things in life where the reality is so wildly removed from the imagination. Two things you can guarantee though – recording is bloody hard work, and drummers are bloody infuriating.

PROMOTING THE BAND — 109

Here we investigate the various different forms of torture the musician will be subjected to in the name of promoting their art, from posters and flyers to photoshoots and video shoots, internet to print media, album launches to merchandise.

PLAYING LIVE — 157

All the best bits about playing in a band happen when you play live, which is what makes it all worthwhile. Unfortunately playing live is also the backdrop to much of the worst bits about playing in a band. No fair.

ON THE ROAD — 195

It's not all dancing around on sweaty stages in front of ambivalent audiences for no money. The other stuff that goes hand-in-hand with playing live mustn't be forgotten – the roadies, the transport, the accommodation, the poor diet and of course the sex and drugs.

THE ROYALTIES — 227

You should get a leaflet with your first instrument explaining how all this stuff works. But you don't. So this chapter might actually be genuinely helpful, unlikely as it may seem if you've made it this far.

ENCORE — 233

Here I reminisce about how much fun I've had on my journey in a desperate but ultimately somewhat futile bid to convince myself I haven't wasted the best years of my life.

GLOSSARY — 237

Not really of much practical use, it's basically a collection of predictable jokes and overt sarcasm. Probably my best work.

ACKNOWLEDGEMENTS — 243

I suppose I better thank these people in case I need their help again.

"Bands, those funny little plans, that never work quite right"

From "Holes" by Mercury Rev

1.
HELLO CLEVELAND!

Being in a band is about the coolest thing you can do for a living. Sure, there are plenty of other cool jobs out there – footballer, actor, astronaut, spy, water-slide tester – and they all have an awful lot going for them, but none of them have quite the full all-round cool game that being in a band does. For example, footballers may be fit, healthy, and exceedingly well paid, but they spend most of their time wearing polyester shorts or tracksuits. And while the actor may well spend half of their life being dressed and styled with the express goal of looking cool - and still be able to do their job with any number of drug habits - you have to ask if their cool is really their own cool, or simply the cool of the person they're *pretending* to be. Astronauts are obviously very cool insofar as they go into space, but this is offset by a heavy quota of nerdiness that is very tough to shake off *and* they're working for The Man. And while James Bond has obviously given the spy a massive cool score, I feel – and hear me out on this one – that just maybe, just perhaps, Mr Bond is not a fair representation of the occupation as a whole. Rather I suspect that presuming all spies are like Bond is akin to thinking all footballers are like George Best.[1] As for water-slide testers, well, it's much harder to pinpoint a weakness in their coolness to be fair, but if there is one I suppose it would be that their coolness is very localised. I mean, being the really cool one in your local pub that everyone points out to their mates before

---

[1] Younger readers ask your Dad. Or Grandad.

whispering *see that chick there, you'll never guess what her job is, she's only a fucking water-slide tester, how cool is that?!* is nothing to be sniffed at, but it's unlikely that your coolness will ever spread much further than this particular pub. To be honest, I'm not even sure it's a job.

Not *every* band is cool of course – being in a covers band does not count at all in any way, shape or form, and being in a tribute act is positively *uncool*. Being in Coldplay certainly disqualifies you. Many heavy metal acts are exempt too, but this is not to mean the genre isn't quite capable as a whole. Ska bands, reggae, jazz, hip-hop, indie, rock, funk – cool man. Hell, there are even some seriously cool traditional folk bands out there these days, no mean feat for a genre whose only really cool exponents for decades were The Dubliners. Scientists have spent many years trying to pinpoint exactly what it is that makes, for example, playing bass for an obscure Japanese lo-fi electro punk band so cool, but thus far they have failed to come up with a universal theory or formula to explain the phenomenon. It's probably something quantum.

It's not playing to large crowds of adoring fans or selling millions of records that makes it so cool. If anything, this has an adverse effect. Many a cool band play shows to well under a hundred people as the norm. Underground bands can in fact make a good case for being the coolest bands of all. And it's not about looking cool, although image is a gateway to coolness and all bands have to have an image – even if that image is having no image. You can get away with dressing in pretty much any manner. *What the hell are you wearing dude? Is that... is that a jumpsuit? Oh this is our new look mate, I'm in a band. Oh wow, that's cool man!* Even just amongst the people I know, all the coolest ones are those that are in, or have been in, bands.[2] But I digress. This isn't supposed to be a dissertation on cool, and I seem to have become entirely distracted from the point of this book from the very start. Sorry.

I grew up in England, in a village near a small home counties town that was pretty much interchangeable with about fifty other almost identical towns. I spent many an hour alone in my room, come rain or shine, listening to records, reading about bands, and standing in front of the mirror pretending to be in a band myself. Aside from the occasional distractions of cricket and football, I dedicated much of my youth to music and imagining how amazing it would be once I had my own band. Thirty years, eight bands, hundreds of gigs and many albums later I feel qualified enough to reveal that, curiously enough, much of what you do when you're in a band is not actually amazing – or cool - in the slightest. Large chunks of it are, in fact, shit. And while the outsider (i.e. the person who is not - and never has been - in a band) has a notion that being in a band is not a job in the true sense and involves a lot of mooching around[3] and very little actual work[4], in reality they have very little idea as to what being in a band actually entails - and what they think they *do* know is mostly wrong. Perhaps this is due to the archetypal modern pop star, shooting to fame in an instant after becoming a popular soap actor or winning some crap TV talent show. Or maybe it's the heavily

---

[2] Although notably they're also the most mentally ill-equipped to deal with life as a whole.
[3] True.
[4] Not true in any way at all.

romanticised portrayal of The Rock Star that's to blame for this, a pervasive notion that successful musicians had a bit of talent, got lucky and now spend all their time snorting cocaine from the naked bodies of famous models, rather than the less romantic reality that they worked their arses off for years for the love of their art at the expense of relationships, family, friends and any sort of physical or mental wellbeing.

Thus one question that all musicians have been asked on numerous occasions is "when are you going to get a real job?", or perhaps its younger sibling "so what do you do for a real job?"[5]. Always this question is asked with a conflicting mixture of scorn and poorly concealed jealousy, although it is arguably a very fair question if you've just seen my band playing to fifteen people and then failing to sell any merchandise. Nevertheless, many people have a curious fascination with the world of the musician, which seems to promise no small degree of riches, decadence and glamour, in return for very little "real" work (I think that for some people, work is only "real" if you hate it).

While it seemed to promise this to me too, upon reflection getting something in writing to that effect would have perhaps been wise. Despite playing in bands since 1989, I've yet to receive any riches, very little glamour, and only minor decadence, and I seem to have

---

5   Another question you'll also get asked repeatedly is something along the lines of "there's a new series of X-Factor soon, why don't you apply for that?". You will entertain notions of punching people that ask this, or perhaps pushing them in front of a bus, but ultimately you'll offer a meek "oh that's not really my thing" and try and quickly change the subject.

done an awful lot of "real" work in the process. Not that this has stopped me from trying, which makes me much like the majority of people that play in bands. Because for every household name, there are another ten fairly well-known bands making a very decent living, and for every ten of these there are another hundred that are making, well, a living. And for every hundred of these, there are thousands upon thousands upon thousands of bands (the 99% if you will) that struggle on year in year out, doing an awful lot of work for very little reward, and doing any number of crap jobs on the side to keep the wolf from the door.

And ultimately we're not doing it for the promise of riches, glamour and decadence. You do meet people at the start who indeed *are* doing it for these reasons, but they all drop out very early on once reality sets in. Those of us who stick at it for many a long year are those that aren't really all that fussed about being cool and glamorous[6], although we'd very much appreciate some of the riches. We're doing it for the love of the music. For the adventure. For those brief but transcendent moments of genuine magic when everything in the universe just clicks together in one beautiful chord. Because we don't really know how to stop. We just keep driving down the road until we break down. And while it's a road to nowhere in particular, the scenery along the way is always worth looking at - even the bits you're looking at it in absolute horror. It's a fucking bumpy old road though.

So what do you do in a band? Well, I decided to write some stuff about it. Perhaps it will help. Some advice; some stories; some

---

6   Which is lucky.

ruminations; some warnings. If you've travelled these roads before, you'll recognise many of the places. If you're not into travelling but you're curious about foreign countries then this might answer some questions. If you're considering setting off on an adventure yourself then this probably won't stop you getting involved in many an accident, but at least you'll know what you're letting yourself in for, get a few handy short cuts, and have an idea what to pack.

2.
LEARNING TO PLAY

As a young kid, I didn't have any family or friends that played an instrument. There were no instruments lying around the house for the curious child to pick up and mess around with. But there was always music to listen to – my Dad had a decent-sized record collection, and he would usually have some tunes on, be it at home or in the car. By the time I was perhaps seven or eight years old I was becoming cognisant of the immense magical power that music holds. I can't think of another artistic discipline that has the power to manipulate one's emotions so intensely in so short a space of time. I spent hour upon hour listening to my Dad's records and subconsciously picking up the methods by which certain songs would send a thrilling chill down my spine. I messed around with writing lyrics before I hit my teens, but for some reason it never dawned on me to actually learn to play an instrument. Looking back now, I think this was probably because it was song-writing that really appealed rather than just the pleasure of playing, say, piano or guitar, but it's equally likely that I may have just been an idiot. I do have a vague memory of receiving a junior guitar one Christmas when I was about eight or nine, a copy of the classic Hank Marvin red and white Stratocaster, but it would be pushing it to describe it as a functioning musical instrument, and it may well have put me off for a bit. Having said that, by the time I was ten I could knock out a respectable version of Three Blind Mice on the recorder, so perhaps I'm underselling myself here.

So I was a relatively late starter as a musician – I didn't get my first proper guitar until I was fifteen, a pearl white electric made by those renowned manufacturers of high-quality instruments, Encore. I think it cost about ninety quid from the local town's only music store. A school friend of mine played guitar, and fifteen-year-old me had something of a belated light bulb moment and thought oh yeah, I could do that, so I did. Like so many misfit teenage boys of the time, growing up just a little too late for punk and instead firmly in the era of synth pop and the new romantics, I'd discovered the joys of loud guitars via the likes of Iron Maiden, AC/DC and Van Halen. Taking the next step and actually becoming the next Eddie Van Halen was the obvious thing to do. I mean, how hard could it be? Turns out it's actually quite hard. And it's certainly very hard to sound like a guitar hero through your ten watt single speaker amp, which only has bass, treble and volume controls. How the hell do you get that distortion sound anyway? Nevertheless, if I wanted to write my own songs and play them, I needed to learn an instrument, and the guitar seemed by far the coolest instrument to learn.

I never had any formal tuition, aside from four or five guitar lessons at the very start from a local guitar teacher. Funnily enough, neither did the vast majority of musicians that I've ever played with. We all generally learned the same way – picking up things from friends, playing along with records, trial and error. Actually reading sheet music was something only for nerds, and nobody with any self-respect was going to do that when you could get the tablature (a sort of music notation for dummies) for Metallica's Ride the Lightening album for five quid. I learnt practically all of my collection of licks and tricks from a cassette tutorial of Twenty Great Angus Young riffs, and never looked back. Over the next year or two I grew out of my heavy metal leanings and found my kindred spirits amongst the punkish rock'n'roll stylings of Johnny Thunders, the Ramones and the Dead Kennedys – which as luck would have it was much, much easier music to play.

Curiously, some of those musicians I've played with over the years who have a formal musical education have been pretty hopeless at playing anything that isn't written out for them. I generally found that the best musicians I played with or associated with were self-taught, with a passion for music that left them with no money, but enormous record collections and an often-encyclopaedic knowledge of the bands and albums they loved. On several occasions I've been looked down upon by sneering trained classical musicians for my almost total inability to read music and explain anything in proper musical language, but then again who really listens to these people? After all, it might sound very impressive to tell people you're playing in an orchestra, but let's face it, you're essentially just playing in a posh covers band - which is only one step above being a DJ. You can't survive on an all-encompassing passion for music alone, but I do think it's the most important weapon in a musician's armoury – far more vital than technical prowess for example. If there's one thing you need more than anything else to get you through the difficult times of playing in a band (i.e. most of them), it's a passion for music. The flip side of that is that it's a damn sight easier to get paying work as a musician when you have, um, technical prowess. In retrospect, and not for the first (or indeed last) time, it's quite possible that I may have severely misjudged the value of actually learning to do something properly.

3.
FORMING A BAND

There's a very good chance your first band will be you and some close friends. There are few more exciting things to do as a teenager than forming a band with your mates. Sure, you'll spend a disproportionate amount of time discussing exactly how famous you will be, arguing over band names, pondering stage clothes and stage moves, dreaming of the expensive gear that one day will be yours, and how great all the sex and drugs will be, but that's all part of the fun and an integral part of the band experience. My first band was formed with three mates from school, and with a whole year's guitar playing under my belt I was by far the most experienced. A drummer who could manage no more than thirty seconds playing before dropping the beat, a bass player with a very pointy bass who was thrash metal mad, and a singer who was too nervous to sing filled out the line-up. I'm sure we must have had a name, but I'm buggered if I can remember it now and while we talked things over to death at school break times, I don't think we ever managed more than a handful of rehearsals. Many burgeoning bands suffer this fate, as once the hard work of writing, rehearsing and being musically competent really kicks in, it is never too long before the cracks begin to show in your glorious plans for world domination.

Every band needs someone that will manage the thing, and that someone will become the boss by default (which makes things difficult in a group of mates – oh look, is that a crack I see?). Usually this will be the person with the most drive, which is also more often than not the person with the most talent and the person who is writing the songs. This person wants to be a success and is prepared to work at it. Which is lucky, as they'll have to work damn hard, for little or no return, with very little help. (It is ironic that the person most important to the music will inevitably be the one who has to spend the most time doing non-musical things, e.g. organising everything and everyone.) If this person is really fortunate, they'll have an ally, perhaps a co-writer, who is prepared to help them spread the load. There are plenty of people out there that enjoy playing music and are quite good at it, that enjoy playing gigs and enjoy being in a band... but who are also unprepared to lift a finger to help run the thing. You will meet these folks, they are everywhere, and at some point you must make a decision as to whether they're worth carrying - as carry them you will. There are always compromises to be made. You'll find yourself mulling over such conundrums as:

- Does Simon's car ownership offset his lack of bass playing ability?
- Anna does tend to forget the words all the time – but she always brings weed to practice.
- Is Matt's talent on the drums worth more than the fact that he's a miserable bastard who brings everyone down at every rehearsal?
- Is Cathy's unreliability and tendency to miss rehearsals worth putting up with given the fact that she brings at least ten mates to every gig?

These become particularly difficult equations when the person in question is also a mate with whom you formed the band. I once had a band made up of myself and two very close friends – Trevor and Den - one of whom, Trevor (drums), worked in tandem with me to run the band, and one of whom, Den (bass)... didn't. The equation we had to solve was does Den's undeniable status as lovely bloke + close friendship + cool looks = +/- his lack of musicality + growing tendency to miss rehearsals to attend meetings at another dodgy pyramid sales scheme he's foolishly got himself involved with. Again. In the end we fired him, a tough call that was clearly a little upsetting for all involved. He heroically covered any emotion by stating that he had to quit soon anyway, as he was going to move to Egypt. Wait, Egypt?! I didn't realise that it was *that* sort of pyramid scheme, cool! I had visions of him moving all his stuff into the King's Chamber of the Pyramid of Khufu in Giza, but in the end he never made the move. Nevertheless, in a fine example of his undeniable lovely bloke/lack of self-respect quota, Den did allow his replacement to borrow his amp and then ended up finding a new role as our roadie. I don't want to give you an unfair impression though – sometimes firing people can be hugely enjoyable. More on that later.

I have vague recollections of another band while I was still at school. I didn't hang around for long, leaving because of good old musical differences – in so far as my so-called best mate (the other guitarist) hated sharing the guitar spotlight with me and wanted me out. Hell, I hadn't even noticed that there was a spotlight. But I did do my first public performance with these guys, an audition for our school dance in front of a handful of judges that didn't like us one bit, and a large proportion of our classmates that also didn't like us one bit. We failed the audition, but curiously I can still recall all the songs we played – cover versions of Nirvana's "Territorial Pissings", Motley Crue's "Dr Feelgood", Bryan Adams' "Summer of 69" and New Model Army's "Get Me Out". After I left, they did a bunch of shows at local parties and such like, filling me with jealousy as I watched on from the sidelines, unable to cash in on the popularity attained by my former comrades. "I used to be in this band you know" is a rubbish chat-up line. I moved on and started my own project forthwith.

You can't continue to play with existing friends for very long. At some point you will need to advertise for somebody to join your band. Either because you wish to improve or expand the line-up, or more likely because somebody leaves - either by their own accord or because you sack them. The same personality clashes that you find in the workplace exist in bands as well, but are generally more problematic, something that is amplified by the fact that musicians are often complete freaks in the first place, and borderline unemployable. In the workplace people might put up with a situation or a colleague that they don't like because at least they're getting paid. Not so in a band. There is rarely a good reason to stick around if you're not enjoying it, and there are always other opportunities to be found. People will continue to drop out for all sorts of reasons. Many people realise pretty quickly that, although it sounded like a great idea at first, being in a band is actually not for them, especially those friends in your first band or two. Some people can't juggle a job and a band. Some will have a family and no longer be able to find the time. Some people have a partner who will insist they leave – "it's me or the band darling, make a choice" is a popular refrain that rarely ends in the band's favour.

Finding a new member is a real minefield. If you're lucky, you already know someone you can ask, perhaps from another band. Poaching feels pretty shitty, but on the Swiss Army Knife of Musician Recruiting, it's definitely an indispensable attachment[7]. Or perhaps a friend knows someone. Word of mouth is a powerful thing. But otherwise it's advertising. In ye olden days that would involve putting up handwritten notices in music stores and rehearsal rooms or paying for adverts in local newspapers and music publications. These approaches can still work now[8] but there are heaps of online options which are probably going to be more effective, and reach more people – although the more people your ad reaches, the more dickheads will apply[9]. And boy oh boy are there some dickheads out there looking to join a band. Urgh.

The majority of wanted ads for musicians are by metal bands. Whether this is because there are more metal bands than other bands or because metal bands have a higher staff turnover than other genres I don't know, but it's undeniably true. And of lot of these will probably be covers bands. I attempted to prove this point to myself in case I had imagined it, by googling musicians wanted and going to the top website on the results. I figured it might be weighting the experiment slightly towards my predicted result if I picked the website's "guitarists wanted" forum, so I plumped for "bassists wanted".

These were the ten most recent adverts:

---

[7] Perhaps the bottle opener, or the corkscrew.
[8] Probably. I haven't had to advertise for musicians for years, so maybe don't take my word for it.
[9] This is an immutable law.

1. Bassist wanted for symphonic black/death metal band

2. Wanted: metalcore bassist

3. Bass player for rock/metal covers band

4. Calling all hard rock bassists!

5. Bassist wanted for metal covers band

6. Bassist needed for thrash metal/industrial project

7. Mysterious bassist required

8. Brand new metal band seeks bass player

9. Bass player to play Sri Lankan Baila

10. Death metal band seeks bassist

See? All but two are metal bands of some form. Number seven caught my eye enough to click on the ad, and although I was still expecting it to be metal related, it was a call out for "someone with a cool dark suave sense of style and an air of mystery about them required to join post-punk/new wave band". As for number nine, well I had no idea what Sri Lankan Baila was, but google tells me it's a unique form of dance that originated among Portuguese fishermen and African slaves during the colonial period – on balance, I'm prepared to give this the benefit of the doubt and categorise it as not metal. I haven't yet run these findings by the Bureau of Statistics, but I'm confident that more rigorous scientific evidence will back me up here.

I once had a temp job that involved me vetting job applications for a company and passing the most promising ones on to the boss for further evaluation[10]. It always surprised me just how many applications were submitted by people that clearly didn't fit the criteria specified in the advert[11] - and musicians wanted ads are no different. If you specify an age range of 18-25, you will get at least one applicant in their forties. If you're after someone with their own transport, you will get an applicant that has no transport (this you will find out half an hour into the initial conversation, just after the point when you've decided they are the ideal candidate). If you specify that your band is influenced by Tom Waits, Leonard Cohen and Lee Hazlewood and you need a percussionist, you will get an applicant who says he is perfect for your band, and who then turns up to the audition in leather trousers and a Slayer t-shirt, and brings a thirteen-piece drumkit with double kick drum. This last example is a common phenomenon, made all the more surprising by the fact that there are so many other bands out there who are actually looking for just that, so how the hell did this dude arrive at your ad?

Once you've begun auditioning you quickly realise a few things. Firstly, auditions are bloody painful. Secondly, you regret not putting in more effort to find a little bit more about the applicant in advance of actually meeting them. Thirdly, wow, there really are an amazing array of different but equally offensive body odours out there. Inviting people to just come down for a jam is an approach that rarely works, and to be honest is probably a little unfair on the applicant. Much better to give them two or three songs to learn – preferably your own

---

10 Hundreds of them, christ it was horrendous.

11 You want an Engineering Production Manager? Brilliant, I've got five years of experience working in a cafe, I'd be perfect!

songs, but if you don't have decent recordings, then ask them to learn a couple of cover versions that your band knows[12]. Apart from making the whole process much more professional, you can soon separate the winners from the losers – and if someone can't be bothered to learn a song properly for an audition, then yes, they're clearly a loser. Likewise, be sure you give them a set time to turn up, even if you're not bothered – because if they're late for the audition then you can guarantee they won't be turning up on time to rehearsal each week either. I once had a guy phone up twenty minutes before an audition to say he couldn't make it, could we do it tomorrow instead (yeah mate, no problem, I'll just pay for tonight's rehearsal room, tell the rest of the band to come back tomorrow and pay for tomorrow night as well). He then called back ten minutes later having realised he was going to blow his chance and said actually he could make it and he was on his way, he'd see us in half an hour – only to then turn up an hour and a half later, while we were auditioning someone else, and get pissed off with us for mucking him around. See? Dickheads everywhere. In contrast the other auditionee had not only learnt the two songs we'd requested, but also about five more from our last album. Job's yours son!

One of my bands desperately needed a new bass player – we'd fired one guy, Mark, essentially for being a miserable bastard that couldn't take a joke, and for refusing to wear anything other than trainers, blue jeans and a black shirt on stage. If nothing else, this is a reflection on our rather misplaced priorities at the time, as Mark was a very decent bass player. And in retrospect, despite feeling great at the time, this

---

12 Every band knows at least a couple of cover versions

was a grievous error. We were never able to really replace him and, as a result, the band lost a lot of momentum, just when we were really hitting our stride. In fact we tried three replacements in quick succession, and every one of the new bass players transpired to have some serious mental health issues[13]. The last of these, a chap by the name of Jake, responded to an ad and we all got together at the singer's house for a cup of tea and a chat. On asking him what sort of stuff he'd played on lately, he promptly pulled out a handful of CDs by one of my favourite bands of the time. WOW. He seemed like a nice guy and was a very good bass player, and he loved our stuff. Perfect! However, as the weeks wore on, it became clear that he had some mental health issues comfortably in excess of those of the previous two incumbents. This culminated in a bizarre gig, which as luck would have it was one of our biggest shows yet, a prestigious support slot to an international touring act. I still have the video footage of the show. Jake starts off just fine, but as the gig goes on and the effects of the alcohol, valium, and God knows what else kick in, you can see him just sort of disintegrate, and he ends up standing there on stage with his arms wide open, looking like a sort of sad and lost indie Jesus, wondering where he is, what to do and what he should be playing. This is not the sort of thing you want in your band, unless you have a very weird band. Things went from bad to worse that night as we were accused by the opening act on the bill of stealing their bass guitar. Well this was fighting talk, as what sort of arsehole band steals another band's equipment? (Actually, quite a few do, but we bloody well didn't!) Fighting talk begets fighting action, and in the end it all kicked off out the back of the venue – it was getting pretty

---

[13] Bear in mind that pretty much every musician has some form of mental health issue, so to have them serious enough to stand out from everybody else means they must be pretty damn bad.

nasty, one of the enemy even punched my girlfriend in the face, until the police arrived and broke things up[14]. This led to us going home and suggesting that under the circumstances we wished that we *had* stolen their bloody bass. Luckily in the morning it turned out that we had. We got a phone call from the police informing us that a certain Jake had been captured on the venue's CCTV camera walking out with the bass guitar in question. Well that was embarrassing. Nice one Jake. I'm not sure what the lesson is here to be honest, other than don't give Jake the bass gig if he turns up to audition for your band. As a curious footnote to this story, I played a solo show some fifteen years later and got chatting to a guy in the audience afterwards. Turned out he was the dude who owned the stolen bass – and in the end he was a bit gutted to get it back, as his Gran had felt so sorry for him that she had offered to buy him a new one!

Thanks to an unlikely chain of events involving a Kiwi, a drug dealer, a reservoir, Paris, a wedding, a deportation, a grass, and a serve of spectacular naivety, I ended up leaving the UK in my mid-twenties, eventually relocating to Australia. When I first arrived down under I had decided to put together a home studio and concentrate on recording, at least as far as my own material was concerned. I wasn't going to get a live band together. Instead I thought that I might look around and see if I could join another band as a guitarist, to satiate my performing needs and to avoid all the inevitable hard work of running my own group. I started checking

---

[14] I must confess that I wasn't involved personally in said fight. Myself and my good friend Richard were enjoying the rare luxury of having a proper band dressing room, and having noted that there appeared to be a surplus of fire extinguishers in there - and no fire - had decided that it was only fair to engage in a fire extinguisher duel. I would never have believed you could fit so much foam in so small a container, but that's science for you.

out the musicians wanted ads myself, and for a long time I could find absolutely nothing appealing whatsoever – after all, I wasn't looking for a metal band. Then I stumbled upon a curious little ad – someone calling themselves Jesus was looking for musicians to form a band and help tell his story. Now for a while I'd been educating myself in the mythology of the world in general, which included the reading of a few books about the famous Jewish carpenter, so this piqued my interest. Ok, so he's probably quite mad, but it's still more intriguing than anything else I've seen in the last six months, so let's see what it's all about. I met up with "Jesus", a thirty-something year old hippy from Byron Bay, complete with dreadlocks and those loose cotton trousers that people from Byron Bay all wear, without exception. I presume it's a legal requirement, or perhaps you get presented with a pair once your dreadlocks reach a certain length. Naturally shoes were out of the question. It turned out that – unbelievably - Jesus wasn't his real name, he was otherwise known as Shane. Shane had been "doing a lot of work on myself" using a meditative technique involving mirrors, which seems incredibly fitting as he was a full-time professional narcissist. Through this work he had come to realise that he was the reincarnation of not only Jesus H Christ, but a certain Adolf Hitler too[15]. Apparently Jesus's reincarnation as Adolf and subsequent genocidal actions were a revenge, a life aimed at getting his own back on the Jews who had been so dastardly to him nearly two thousand years previous. His current incarnation – Shane – was here to reconcile the two previous personalities and bring peace across the world via the medium of improvised music[16]. I quite liked Shane, but this all seemed a little improbable if I'm honest, especially the last bit. Shane was purifying himself and would no

---

15 I've often wondered what the H stood for, amd now I find myself wondering if the H is for Hitler.

16 God works in mysterious ways.

longer drink alcohol or smoke weed, although I soon worked out that what he actually meant was he would no longer drink alcohol or smoke weed *unless it was someone else's*. Anyway, more out of morbid fascination than anything else, I had a few jams with him[17]. I would "improvise" some guitar, which would at least half of the time mean playing around with riffs from songs I knew he wouldn't recognise as I couldn't think of anything better to do. He would then sing his story over the top, with a deep strong voice that was genuinely powerful and affecting[18] - although how he'd have felt if he knew his emotional outpourings were being accompanied by the riff from Animal Nitrate by Suede, a song about gay sex and poppers, I don't know. At first I was quite impressed by the range of melodies that Shane/Hitler/Jesus could improvise. Then he asked me if he could have a go on my guitar, so he started noodling away and I started singing. I realised at this juncture that it is actually incredibly easy to sing any old nonsense along to someone playing guitar, and in fact this is the way I write songs anyway – the difference being that in the process of writing you cast aside all the crap and keep the good bits, and really fine tune the lyrics. I suggested as such, along with the notion that perhaps we should just make these stories into songs, but Shane wasn't impressed. It just wouldn't be pure, man[19]. It was within about five minutes of ending this last rehearsal that I realised if I wanted a half-decent band then the only option was to form my own one. I think I was one of the first disciples that Shane recruited, but I was by no means the last. I would sometimes see adverts for gigs he was doing, but I never made it along to one. Fair play to the dude though, he stuck at it and gave it a really good go. I know the plan was

---

17   One session of which I recorded, and still have. It's actually very good at times!

18   Well this make sense of course, as both Jesus and Hitler were clearly very good public speakers.

19   And we know all about his previous incarnation's views on purity.

to be touring the world in 2013 with a twelve-piece band (of course!), but to the best of my knowledge this never happened, even though this was prophesised by Shane himself many years previously.

I've lost count of the number of godawful auditions I've been part of, but every now and then you meet someone that fits the bill perfectly. I met up with a young music teacher, Sally, who had expressed an interest in joining my band. I'll always ask a candidate who their favourite band is, and ask them to name a couple of their favourite songs too[20]. Now you don't need someone to like the same stuff as you, but it really helps if they at least get where you're coming from. This can be particularly tricky if, like me, you emigrate to the other side of the world and find that practically nobody you meet has ever heard of the music that's inspired and influenced your own. It also helps if they don't say they love symphonic death metal (unless of course you are a symphonic death metal band). Don't forget, at some point you'll probably be sharing a tour bus/car with them and listening to their choice of music for a while – and driving long distances with someone whose entire music collection seems to consist of angry shouting over loud guitars and bad string samples, is rubbish, trust me. I suspect you're probably quite happy to trust me on this as some truths are fairly self-evident. But in Sally's instance, she gave answers to the questions very much alike to the answers I'd give if asked myself. Hooray! The feeling of joy and relief in these rare instances is to be savoured like a fine wine.

---

20 It's amazing how many musicians struggle to answer this.

Getting the right line up is a curious thing. If you're the one running the band – which as I mentioned earlier will normally mean you're the one writing the songs, booking the rehearsals, arranging the gigs, designing the posters, constructing the website, arranging recordings and basically doing (and paying for) pretty much everything – then you need an ally. They don't need to do all that much in reality, but if you find someone that can, for example, arrange the rehearsals for you, it makes a huge difference to your own personal workload and headspace. With a decent ally in the ranks, you can quite easily put up with, say, a rhythm section that do nothing outside playing their own instruments as required. In fact, if someone turns up on time and pays their share of rehearsals, does their homework and isn't a complete twat, then consider that a major win. Often you don't want the help per se (if you want something done properly, do it yourself...), but what you *do* want is an absence of bloody hassle.

One of the best allies I had was a guitarist by the name of Spider. I'd chanced upon Spider's band online a few days after writing a song about an obscure and vaguely local folk story. I was pretty chuffed to have written this song - only to discover that his band had already recently done the same thing, but better. Nevertheless, I got in touch and he ended up adding his guitar to a few songs on an album we were working on, and this in turn led to me asking him to join the band on a permanent basis. This proved a revelation. For the first time in years, I gained myself a brilliant musician, a co-writer, someone that booked decent gigs with no help or prompting at all, someone that would happily drive around the city with me at 1am on a Monday night with a bunch of posters and a bucket of wallpaper paste. Also, somebody who actually bought their own weed. Someone like this is invaluable (you can never have enough back-up dealers), although they will cause problems with the rest of the band who quickly build up enmity towards the new member as they're making them look distinctly second class. Which indeed happened very quickly in this case. The line-up had been ambling along nicely enough for a couple of years but was not to last much longer. All of a sudden everything became about the music, which was something of an issue to those who once away from the stage were far more interested in X-rated playing cards, shit TV and bad fantasy novels. So the music and the writing moved on exponentially and the gigs got bigger and better, and when you reach this stage it becomes clear which people are in the band for a bit of fun and which people are doing it with their heart and soul. At which point something's got to give.

Which brings us back to firing people. As I mentioned before, it can be a horrible thing if that person is a good mate who just isn't up to the job. If, however, it's somebody that's been bugging you for a while and you've finally decided you've had enough, pulling the trigger can be extraordinarily satisfying. Going back to the situation above, Spider was not proving popular with two other members of my band. Now in fairness said pair were genuinely nice people, always there for rehearsals and always paying their way, and that is a fair bit of what you need in a musician. They were also very committed to certain aspects of the band. Unfortunately, those aspects were not really the music, rather they were a commitment to searching eBay for tasteless stage clothes, and flirting with each other interminably. If all that shopping enthusiasm and frustrated sexual energy could have been channelled into the music, it could have been really something. When they both teamed up and threatened to leave if that bloody guitarist isn't fired, it was with no small sense of delight that I told them they were sacked. My delight only increased when I realised that being sacked themselves was clearly not a possibility they'd entertained when hatching their coup.

A good indicator of how committed a former band member is to the general musical cause is what they do after you've fired them. If they live and breathe music then they'll be forming their own band or joining a decent existing band quick sharp. In the case of the duo above, after a brief spell in a really, really bad metal band[21], one turned to soft-porn fetish modelling and the other, coincidentally, to soft porn fetish photography. This sort of afterlife study is an infallible indicator as to whether or not you did the right thing.

Sometimes firing somebody can be hard for unexpected reasons. In one case of mine, this was because somebody didn't realise they'd been fired. I still don't quite know how they didn't work it out to be honest, although if, as I did, you actually like the individual whom one must fire (the firee?), one does tend to beat around the bush a little. The conversation went something like this:

"Listen dude, we've been doing this together for eight years now, but it's come to the stage where I need a change of approach, something different"

"Ok, yeah"

---

[21] To be fair, as we've already discovered, statistical studies do seem to show that if you're looking for a new band, most of your options will be metal.

"It's been good fun, but I've decided to move on, and do things differently with the band"

"Right, sure"

"So it's really hard for me to say this, but I have decided to end our partnership and play with some other people"

"Yeah I get ya"

"Sorry mate, it's nothing personal I just feel like it's run it's natural course and I need a change"

<pause>

"So, are we rehearsing next week?"

But painful though ending a relationship like this can be, the relief is palpable once it's done – if there is one thing I learnt far too late in the game, it was to be ruthless in pursuit of what you want, rather than shirking the difficult decisions by avoiding confrontation. Embrace your inner bastard and learn to love that confrontation – the band is only ever as strong as its weakest link.

People will often leave bands out of the blue, sometimes for the strangest reasons, and you never see it coming. I had a duo with a guy from Scotland, Will. Lovely chap, hugely talented, very quiet and unassuming - wouldn't say boo to a ghost. We did a bunch of shows and everything was ticking along nicely. I was just getting ready to leave the house for a local gig when I got a phone call from his wife:

"Will's not going to be able to make the show tonight"

"What is he sick or something? Tell him to toughen up ha ha"

"No... <sob> he's been arrested"

"Arrested? Will?! What on earth for?!"

"Bigamy <sob>"

"Um... say that again?

"Bigamy. He's got two other wives!"

Turned out that one of the previous wives had a very unimpressed father who was also very well connected, and although it took some years, once they finally tracked Will down, he was arrested and thrown in jail. Sometimes, they never see it coming either.

Bringing in new members to a band that's already a well-oiled machine comes with its own disadvantages. If you have a few albums out, a load of tours under your belt, you can attract a better standard of musician. That's good right? Yes, it is. Mostly. I got me some new members and for a year or so was able to pay them a decent amount for each show (by which I mean I was able to pay them for each show). They'd bypassed the previous eight long years of doing the hard yards with this band and not getting paid, which is what had got the band to the stage where the members could earn money. But there wasn't enough to pay people *and* put some money aside for anything other than travelling and accommodation expenses. The problem then arose of how to record another album.

"Hasn't the band got any money?"

"No mate, we've taken most the money ourselves as pay"

"Well how are we going to get the money for the studio then?"

"Well, I have a few shows I can line up – if we put all the money back into the band, after a month or two we'll be able to record another album"

"So we won't get paid for the gigs?"

"Not personally, no"

"Well I'm not doing them then"

Sigh. The problem here of course is that without a new product, you can't keep booking shows, and even if you can then you won't have any new product to sell anyway. So... you're kinda stuck, basically. In this instance, it was one of several proverbial straws that broke the camel's back, helping nobody.

In more recent times I've not bothered with a band. I was gigging less and less, and apart from a semi-regular companion playing fiddle I was on my own. Ah, sweet bliss. When shows came up that necessitated a band, I simply hired them for the job in hand. I'd reached a stage where I knew enough good musicians who could help out as required and was earning just about enough from the gigs to pay them appropriately. The first time I did a gig in this manner I was so surprised at the ease of it all that I had to sit down and have a long hard drink about things. I wrote out a setlist for the shows we would play that weekend a month or so in advance, and asked all musicians involved to learn them accordingly. Then I met them all at my place on the morning of the first show, did one quick run through of the set in my lounge room and went off to the festival. The shows went superbly, and I recall not a single screw up by anyone concerned. Well this is more like it I thought. I mean, sure, there's something to be said for the regular band and all that it entails, but the notion that I could just turn up and do a great gig with a band after a solitary one hour rehearsal (which to be honest we could have got away with not doing) was something of a revelation. I suppose this is what it's like for the more successful musicians all the bloody time, except they probably have someone else to send the musicians the songs to learn and don't bother with the quick jam in my lounge[22]. After thirty-plus years of this stuff, I've been forced to conclude that many people that play in bands are absolute chancers, unwittingly holding back bands with their own disbotherance. And once you reach the stage of being able to attract a certain quality of musician, things get exponentially easier for all concerned. But where's the fun in that?

---

[22] I wouldn't let them in anyway.

4.
WRITING A SONG

I recall writing my first song, some years before I learnt to play guitar. I was about twelve years old, and in the best folk tradition I stole the tune from someone else - in this case the Simple Minds song "Alive and Kicking" - and wrote a set of my own lyrics to it, which thankfully no longer exist. If this doesn't count – and I'm happy to admit there's a strong case that it doesn't – then I reckon I was sixteen when I wrote the first song that was entirely my own work. By which I mean I composed both lyrics and music, although by "composed" I *really* mean "ripped off a Dogs D'Amour song". Nevertheless, the feeling of creating my own song was thrilling, and to be honest that thrill of creating a new song is still every bit as strong thirty years later - although I no longer feel the need to imitate The Dogs D'Amour.

Song writing is a funny thing[23], and the more you do it the more you realise what an absolute gift it is to be able to write a simple catchy three chord pop song – far, far harder than writing an eight-minute epic complete with tempo changes and seventeen different chords. I

---

[23] Unless, ironically, you write comedy songs, in which cased it's usually some considerable distance away from funny (although I'll grant an exception to this rule for a very small number of comedy songs, including Apu's "Who Needs a Kwik-E-Mart" tune, which is an absolute cracker, and anything by David O'Doherty.

reckon the best way to learn the art of song writing is to learn other people's[24] songs, see how they've done it and then steal their ideas, while mixing in just enough of your own ideas to fool people in to thinking it's all your own genius. This is a tried and tested formula used by the very best of song writers throughout time - no matter how much some songsmiths like to deny it.

While it's certainly something you can learn, I'm undecided as to whether song writing is something you can actually teach. On the one hand, everything should theoretically be teachable in some way. But I've read a couple of books that aim to do just that with regards writing a song, and they were awful. I don't think you can put rules to a creative process, but that doesn't stop people from trying. I've also been to a couple of song writing workshops at festivals, and these have struck me as almost entirely useless as well. Then again, speaking as someone who has written and recorded hundreds of songs and scored precisely zero hits, my opinion is probably at best politely ignored, and at worst deserving of nothing but scorn. And there are of course many rules to music theory itself – ignore them at your own peril. An old friend used to scoff at my refusal to learn the rules, on the basis that if you *know* the rules it's a lot easier to break them. You should probably listen to him.

As mentioned previously, the song writer in the band is usually the person doing all the other work of running the band too. Most bands will have one writer, although of course there are lots of successful

---
[24] By other people I'm thinking of the likes of David Bowie, Bob Dylan or Kate Bush, not your mate Greg.

writing partnerships too – Jagger & Richards and Lennon & McCartney being some of the most famous song writers to have ever lived. Co-writing is a funny thing. I wrote a number of songs with my mate Robbie that were total collaborations from the bottom up and this is the only time I've worked in this manner – and the songs we wrote together bore little in common with what we wrote individually, which was a hugely rewarding experience. But further down the track I also co-wrote with my guitarist Spider, and this simply involved him tarting up my pretty much finished songs, perhaps by adding a middle eight or changing the odd chord while bemoaning the fact that I'd written yet another bloody song in A-minor.

What you will undoubtedly experience before too long is the band member who insists you play one of *their* songs, in fact in the interests of fairness shouldn't we all chip in with a few songs, I mean you've written the whole set mate and that's not really fair at all is it, after all we're all chipping in cash for rehearsals? I've had a few people make a suggestion along these lines, and a general rule of thumb seems to be that the shittier their songs are, the harder they push to have them included. Now the odds of having one decent songwriter in a band are slim enough, but the chances of having several are absurdly slim. I can think of only one decent example – The Moody Blues. In their late sixties/early seventies heyday, their albums were made up of songs composed (usually individually, rather than co-written) by all five band members, all of whom were very good song writers. But this is not to mean you should take this as a template for your band, as it will not work. Really, it won't. The only other example that springs to mind[25] is Crosby, Stills, Nash and Young – and look how well that turned out. Funnily enough, the one time I had a really good songwriter in my band (the aforementioned Spider), he was appalled at the possibility that we play some of his songs - Spider suffering from a chronic crippling self-doubt that made my own self-doubt seem positively motivational.

Something I find curious is the number of writers who write some quite astonishingly good stuff at a very early age, but seem incapable of keeping the standard up as they get older. Jagger & Richards are a great example of this. Does the muse simply move on elsewhere, having done the job? Does huge success kill the motivation to continue? Do they simply lose the knack? Do drugs wreck the creative talent? One indisputably brilliant writer - David Bowie – had lengthy periods where he seemed utterly incapable of writing anything remotely in the same class as his earlier work, yet in later years he seemed to very much find his gift again. Some writers seem to age like a fine wine – Nick Cave's writing seems to get better and better, and the same could be said of Tom Waits.

So what constitutes writing a song? There are three main components – the lyrics, the chord sequence, and the melody. If I'm writing a song, these three components will all be written at the same time, by me. I can't help but write them all at the same time, that's just how it seems to happen. On a handful of occasions I've come up with a complete lyric on its own and added the music later,

---

25 Yeah, I could research this properly, but that would run the risk of spoiling my argument.

but I find it most natural to construct the whole edifice at the same time. Other people work differently, Elton John for instance being a famous example of someone who writes very little in the way of lyrics – Bernie Taupin providing them more often than not. But this sort of arrangement tends to be the exception rather than the rule. What does *not* constitute writing part of the song is the instrumentation itself. But you can be sure that some band members you meet, almost certainly the same ones that want you to play their songs too, will insist that they deserve a writing credit because they wrote the bass line. Or the drum part, guitar part etc etc. They will steadfastly refuse to acknowledge that their contribution is in any way less important than yours, the actual writer of the song. This argument is of course wrong on many levels, not least the fact that you could have got anyone to put a bass line on the song and it would still be the same song. In fact, the song exists essentially unchanged without any bass at all. And if you hadn't written the song in the first place, they would never have written that bass line. Now if they have written a bass line which has inspired you to write a song around it then that's a different kettle of fish entirely, but writing a bass line for an already written song is not the same thing as writing the actual song. It is, in fact, simply writing a bass line. But I've met a few people who simply aren't prepared to accept this, two who actually left bands as a result, feeling like they were being conned out of royalty payments – which apart from being entirely wrong, was something of a moot point when the royalties amounted to perhaps 3 pence a year.

Aside from the writing of the song itself, there is also the arrangement, and this is commonly where your non-song-writing buddies may well get themselves a credit[26]. The arrangement is simply the way the song is, um, arranged. The clue is in the word arrangement. The lyrics, melody and chords constitute the writing of the song, but it's common for the whole band to play around with different arrangements of the song until it all gels – perhaps adding in another chorus, changing the length of an instrumental break etc. You've probably seen song credits that look something like this – *trad, arr by Smith/Bloggs* – indicating that the songs itself is a traditional folk song, such as Whiskey In The Jar, but the arrangement of said song was done by Smith and Bloggs, i.e. they've taken a traditional song written by someone else and arranged their own take on it, earning themselves a credit in the process.

Some bands will just split everything right down the middle, regardless of who wrote what. This is only really an option if the band has remained unchanged throughout its life, and will usually be a group of friends only too happy to operate as some form of socialist collective, but if one or two people leave then everything suddenly starts getting very messy. U2 do it this way I believe. I'm not sure if this works as a motivational tool to encourage everybody involved to give it their all, or a demotivational tool to encourage people to think sod it, I get paid the same regardless, I'll just go through the motions. I'll resist the temptation to make a judgement on this based on U2's output.

---

26 In other words, some cash. Or in some other words again, the potential of some cash at some undetermined point in the future, that will in all likelihood never eventuate.

Overall I reckon it's definitely a wise idea to have a conversation with your band about these issues as early in the piece as possible, as it can be a source of friction further down the line. Perhaps sign an agreement of some sort if you can really be bothered. Yet another thing to take up your time that could be better spent writing songs...

5.
THE REHEARSAL ROOM

Most of us have started off rehearsing in the same sort of space – a parent's lounge room or garage being the beginners eternal go-to favourite. This is not a long-term option however, as generally most parents have something known as neighbours. Even if you or a fellow band member is lucky enough to have parents prepared to put up with the infernal racket you are almost certainly making at this stage, you can be sure their neighbours are not. Yes, it's a mildly amusing novelty at first, but three Saturday afternoons in a row of hearing your neighbour's offspring butchering AC/DC songs at full volume is enough to test the patience of the kindest soul. Basically, work on the assumption that you have one free rehearsal at the home of each member of the band that you can use up before you must start to look elsewhere.

So what you're looking for is a dedicated rehearsal space. Initially that doesn't necessarily mean an actual proper grown-ups rehearsal studio. Any space will do (so you think), so you end up trying your luck with a variety of local places that may fit the bill – a village hall, a church hall, a scout hut, you get the idea. Usually these places are available for free, or are very cheap, and they're local. These are both essential criteria for a rehearsal space at this stage because you're probably still at school and (a) have no money (get used to that), and (b) you need your parents to drive you there. However, these places all tend to have one thing in common – an almost complete lack of convenient power outlets, and no facilities for a musician whatsoever. By this I don't mean toilets or a kettle, I mean a PA system. You don't have one yourselves of course as you could only just afford your crappy guitar and amp, and you're not even quite sure what the PA does. This doesn't bother the budding drummer, guitarist or bass player for a moment, but you realise the importance as soon as anyone wants to sing, or play an instrument that may not necessitate its own amplifier but does need a mic and a PA system in a band environment – trumpet, violin, didgeridoo etc. This problem is compounded by the fact that usually these types of rehearsal space have bloody appalling acoustics – polished wooden floors and glass windows are a fantastic way of making instruments that are usually unbearably loud (drummers and guitarists I'm looking at you) even fucking louder. So you need a PA system capable of getting a vocal to cut through this noise – and it most definitely is noise – and they don't really exist within the realms of affordability. The cheaper make-do options include plugging in that quality microphone the singer purchased from Aldi into a guitar amp, which *will* sound awful. No matter what you do. Why can't I just get the musicians to turn down their amps I hear you say? Well, granted, I suppose it is *technically* possible. But with the best will in the world there's not a lot you can do to make drums quiet. Actually that's not true. It's easy to make the drums quiet, you simply fire the drummer. This is an appealing solution in so many ways, but with some major drawbacks. It's better perhaps to bow to the inevitable and move on…

So what you really need is a *proper* dedicated rehearsal room. There are varying levels of quality out there, and as with most things you'll generally get what you pay for. This is a lesson you should learn as early as possible. Personally I doggedly refused to learn this lesson for many years. Don't be like me. I remember the first proper rehearsal room I hired with my first band. This is a surprisingly exciting moment. It was about ten quid for a three-hour slot, and had a vocal PA, loosely speaking. *This* was more like it. And close enough to home to mean lifts from parents were feasible. It was indubitably right at the bottom of the rehearsal room league table – fighting relegation to be honest – but it was still a better rehearsal room than we were a band. Then again, it was a sideline for the farmer that owned the land, and I think that this possibly wasn't his area of expertise, even with the best will in the world. It was a rather dilapidated old brick building in the countryside that had seen much better days – the building equivalent of an old Ford Escort rotten through with rust and sitting on a pile of bricks in an overgrown garden next to a broken washing machine, a wicker chair with a hole where the seat once was, and a fridge with no door. Several things about it have stuck in my memory: the Teenage Mutant Ninja Turtles curtains, the woeful attempt at soundproofing by nailing about six egg cartons to the wall, and the slightly unnerving feel of the place. But, to its major credit, it did have a stage-shaped, slightly raised area at the end of the room, so you could pretend you were on stage being a proper musician - a hugely important feature for the budding rock star – and a PA that worked okay maybe thirty percent of the time. I later found out that the building had formerly been a prisoner of war camp that used to hold enemy soldiers in World War 2, which goes someway to explaining the unsettlingly eerie vibe of the place. Although as we were knocking out piss poor versions of early Metallica songs, I reckon any ghostly inhabitants were staying as far away as possible.

Rehearsal rooms on farms seem to be a bit of a theme for me. Once I had my own transport, I upgraded to a new rehearsal room... on a farm. You would drive through the mud of the farm to the back of a cattle shed, where a little room was tacked on the end. But - and this is an important but - this one was run by a musician, a likeable chap called George. Inside the cattle shed the walls were padded out and covered in white sheets[27]. The room was cosy, but had several mics and stands, power outlets, wall mounted speakers and a PA that worked fine at least fifty percent of the time. It felt like a proper rehearsal room anyway. On the whole though, I recommend not rehearsing on farms. Smell can be an issue, and I once made the mistake of inviting a journalist from the local paper to a rehearsal. They wanted to do a photoshoot with us next to an old tractor trailer, as "it would look like we were really going places"[28]. Predictably the place fell to pieces when George got out and, yes, the farmer took over the business.

Still, there's always the slim chance that you may one day find yourself in a position of Being Proper Lucky[29] and get yourself a half-decent free rehearsal room, something of a holy grail for young bands in their formative years. I twice found myself in this position and, thinking back, at the time I was entirely too inexperienced to know the value of what I had. After leaving school and living for a

---
27 White-*ish*
28 Yeah, mainly to somewhere else on the farm.
29 There are many varieties of Being Proper Lucky that can occur. I have a feeling that if you get them all at the same time, you will be A Huge Success.

few years on dole money and occasional cash in hand jobs, I had to get a regular job. Mysteriously I was yet to ink a major record deal, but in the meantime I took part-time employment with a small company on a local industrial estate. One of the other chaps that worked there was also a musician, Brian, and he had his own very decent PA system[30]. This PA was stored in the small warehouse next to the office[31], and he rehearsed there with his rockabilly band some evenings. After I'd been in the job a while, I too was able to use this facility[32]. We lined up in a row in the long thin space by the back door, surrounded by shelves stacked with roller bearings. It wasn't the perfect rehearsal space, but it was free and available six nights a week without bookings, and it's hard to overstate the importance of this[33]. To be honest, the cramped conditions made for better acoustics. I could get away with leaving our drums and amps there too[34], and we could make as much noise as we liked[35]. In retrospect, perhaps it was the perfect rehearsal space[36]. A word of warning though – when you're actually paying for a space, you tend to make the most of your time there. When you're not paying for a room, it's much easier to fuck around a bit and take it for granted, especially when you can - to give a complete fictional example that I've made up on the spot and that certainly never actually happened - get into the office and use the computer which has a multi-player golf game on it and before you know it you're all embarking on a lengthy PC-based golfing tour of the world and getting your handicap down to professional levels, at the expense of the band.

---

30 This is also Being Proper Lucky.
31 As is this.
32 Yep, this too.
33 So is this.
34 Dude, seriously?
35 Man, I really squandered this lucky streak.
36 <insert regret here>

After a year or so I'd left this job, but found myself rehearsing for free again[37], just a street away at a place where, remarkably, regular full-time employment had actually been given to my bass player Den[38], much to everyone's surprise. Including Den's. We needed our own PA, so I bought myself a cheap (duh) vocal PA head, and built a couple of small speaker cabinets with two speakers from a knackered old guitar amp and some scraps of wood. What it lacked in volume it made up for with poor tone and faulty reverb. Anyway, the company that owned our new rehearsal room made road signs, and this is a real bonus if you're the sort of band (hint: you are. All of you.) that thinks it would be cool to mark any amps, flight-cases, bass drums etc with heavy duty machine-cut reflective stickers in all manner of bright colours. They also employed another guy, Jim, who also played bass[39], and when we subsequently sacked Den[40] in favour of Jim, we were able to continue to rehearse at the same spot. Yeah baby, luck was on my side. For a while anyway.

Another word of warning here – rehearsing at a place of work can also mean attracting other people that also work there. In this instance, that means a psychologically unbalanced hard-as-nails drug-dealing motor-cycling speed-freak lesbian who, after an initial period of volunteering some useful electrical help with equipment, roadie/security services and some supplies of assorted substances, went a bit mad(der) and amongst other things kidnapped my girlfriend and threatened to drown her in a reservoir, and hung around the

---

37 No, really!
38 Yes, you are remembering correctly – I did sack Den, but that was in the previous band, and then he joined me again in my next band.
39 I think I used up my lifetime Being Proper Lucky quota within about 6 months, before I even realised I had it. I'm an idiot.
40 Inevitably.

bedroom window of my ground floor flat at night with a big hammer.

Talking of unwanted people – we rehearsed a couple of times in the back room of a local pub. On the last occasion a punter walked into the back room, stood listening and visibly thinking hard for a few seconds, then went up to my amp and adjusted the sound, which went from poor but acceptable copy of Johnny Thunders to possibly the worst guitar sound I've ever heard. Then walked off. What the fuck?

The more I think about this, the more I realise what strange locations I rehearsed in. I don't know if it's the same everywhere for everyone, but I like to think so. For a while I rehearsed in a room on an old British Aerospace rocket testing site. They no longer tested there, and some of the old buildings were now rented out as a result, although you still had to enter the site via a security checkpoint and be approved for admittance – not always a given. It was so fucking cold there that playing your instrument was genuinely difficult, but at least there was plenty of parking on the enormous disused rocket testing runways (which also enabled you to test the top speed of your car, which I think can be considered a not inconsiderable bonus). After the cold scared us away, the band found a room in a disused flour mill. It was ok – a reasonable PA that worked at least seventy-five percent of the time, a service station across the road for refreshments, and some decent urban decay to utilise for band photos. It was at the bottom of a building about seven stories high, but with no roof. We rehearsed there on the last occasion after a steady period of rain, which had flooded the upper levels and caused havoc with the electrics. When

I plugged my guitar in, the resultant electric shock was enough to throw me off my feet several metres backwards and right that's it guys, I'm not rehearsing here again thank you very much.

Eventually you figure that a bit more money in exchange for a decent room with good sound is, on balance, probably worth it. Hell, it's almost as if you get what you pay for. Proper rehearsal rooms were few and far between where we were based, but there was one within half an hour of us that wasn't bad. By which I mean it had several rooms available, all sound proofed and equipped with PAs that worked at least ninety percent of the time and <gasp> had someone on hand to help you if (well, when) the PA broke down.

But finding a decent rehearsal room is only half the battle. You also need one that is available on the night/s that you want, every week. Having a place with several rooms doesn't necessarily make this any easier, as they'll have a bigger client base. What you can absolutely rely on is that when you all finally come to an agreement on which night you rehearse each week, you won't be able to book a room anywhere on that night for love nor money, and rehearsing will become a constant juggling act of checking availability week after week. When after six months of pissing around you finally get everything running smoothly on a Wednesday night, take this as a sign that within the next couple of weeks somebody will unexpectedly leave the band, and the next person to join will work on Wednesday nights. Incidentally, despite having seven days you can choose from, getting a group of young musicians to rehearse on Friday nights (yeah right mate), Saturday nights (are you kidding me?), Sunday nights (urgh, really?)

and even Mondays (well if we have to, but I'd rather not) can be a problem. This is why rehearsal rooms are nearly always booked out well in advance on Tuesdays, Wednesdays and Thursdays. Of course, if you're not working a regular job then daytime becomes an option, but then you're back to the problem of not being able to afford a proper rehearsal room anyway.

A decent sized city is likely to have a few rehearsal places that are actually pretty good, although they're costly. I was nearing thirty before I moved to a big international city and discovered a new world of rehearsal facilities – places that had vending machines, places that sold spare strings, straps, leads etc, even a place with an onsite weed dealer and a dog. Okay, it wasn't a very friendly dog, but pats were on offer if you were careful. I've even discovered places with pool tables and licensed bars, and great though this seems, it's not necessarily good for the wallet or the productivity. Even so, these places can be prone to the same risks as their lesser cousins, and also come with new and unexpected problems – what do you mean our room is up those stairs? What do you mean there's no unloading bay and the nearest car park is a ten-minute walk away? And one of life's certainties is that even in the best rehearsal rooms, most of the mic stands will, after many years of abuse, be a bit shit, and will swing around on their own accord, or lower themselves at random, or not fit the microphone securely. Or more likely all of the above. But you can at least fix the mic stand, presuming you packed the gaffer tape.

Talking of which, this seems as good a point as any to properly introduce our good friend gaffer tape. It was invented by filmmaker

Ross Lowell in 1959, and Ross is an absolute hero to all musicians, even if they've never heard of him. Gaffer tape is the single most important item in any bands armoury, and also one of the cheapest. You can't afford not to have it. Basically gaffer tape is like The Force – it has a dark side, a light side, and binds the universe together. There are very few things that cannot be fixed with gaffer tape, and lest you think I'm rather over-selling it, consider this little list of things I've used it for: fixing microphone stands, stopping my guitar strap falling off mid-song, sticking plectrums to my guitar, mending my boot, sticking plectrums to my mic stand, substitute (and superior) band-aid, mending a cracked drum stool seat, fixing a hole in the van's exhaust pipe, tidying cables on stage, holding a lead securely in my guitar, binding a drumstick to my drummer's injured hand, extending the life of battered flight-cases by several years, fixing dodgy wiring in leads, holding my finger together after an accident with tent pole, holding a tent pole together after an accident my with finger, fixing setlists to the stage, support for a sprained ankle, temporary sling for an injured arm, mending a hat, re-attaching a bumper to the van, a makeshift speaker stand, a stand for tilting monitor and amplifier, mending a tear in trousers, dampening the sound from drums, repairing a torn speaker cone, marking spots to stand on for video shoots, removing pet hair from black stage clothes, manufacturing an emergency belt substitute, affixing merchandise to venue walls, fixing gels onto stage lights, an on-stage beer holder, labelling channels on mixing desks, affixing radio mics to straps, making a temporary football, adding a go-faster stripe to the van, fixing broken battery clips on guitar effects pedals, emergency book binding, making a temporary rope, repairing glasses, fixing a strap on a violin case and – perhaps most importantly - creating enormous graffiti (gaffiti?) on a dressing room wall. Note that this list does not include the vast number of things I've used it for outside of the band environment. Buy it. Keep it with you. At all times. And be mindful of the fact that it's by far the most likely item of your band's possessions to be stolen!

But back to the rehearsal room. In another rain related incident, one regular rehearsal room I used was flooded the day before we were in, and the resulting smell was unbearable. The carpet was still squelching for God's sake. And I hear tell that, generally speaking, water and electricity shouldn't be mixed. These rooms will not have any windows or air circulation, and the floor and ceiling will be carpeted, along with padded walls. In short, not places that will dry out quickly – if at all - when flooded. Rehearsal rooms smell pretty bad at the best of times, damp rehearsal rooms are truly an experience to avoid at all costs. After a few hours in this one I felt notably nearer death than I felt beforehand, and I swear my lungs were actually growing mould by the end of the session. Naturally we were charged full price - in fact we were told that if we didn't wish to use the room that night we would be subject to a cancellation fee!

Sound-proofing at rehearsal rooms is patchy, one might even say optional. I understand this, as genuine sound-proofing is a very expensive process, but sound-bleed from the band in the next room is nearly always a problem. And another immutable law of the universe is that the worse a band is, the louder they play. And the louder they play, the more likely they are to be a metal band. Now I have no objection to metal bands per se – they're mostly normal people like you or I, just with worse dress sense. But the band you can hear above the volume of your folk-rock combo, or your indie-pop trio, or your jazz-fusion quartet will *always* be a bunch of long-haired musicians dressed in black jeans and wearing black t-shirts with some form of skull motif. Expect to be drowned out by an interminably long, loud and dull noise fest with several tempo changes, or a selection of covers of songs by Iron Maiden, Black Sabbath, Motley Crue, Metallica and Guns'n'Roses. Or whatever their modern day equivalents are. I'm rather out of touch with regards the metal bands of the 21st century.

When all is said and done, I thoroughly enjoy the experience of rehearsing at an actual rehearsal room. But it's worth weighing up the pros and cons, and understanding that there is an awful lot to be said for turning into a folk band and rehearsing acoustically in the warm, pleasantly scented comfort of your home, and the bar is generally much cheaper.

6.
BOOKING A GIG

The best thing about being in a band is doing a brilliant gig. They're not all brilliant by a long stretch, but those that are make it all worthwhile. But *booking* gigs is shit. It's a shit job that too often results in shit gigs. I'd like to leave it at that frankly, but that'll help no one, so I shall endeavour to share some of my vast experience of this most shitty of all the shitty jobs that go with being in a band!

When I first started trying to get gigs, it was actually fairly easy. Well less hard anyway. This was in the early nineties, when live music in pubs and clubs was still a reasonably popular form of entertainment. After all, television was a handful of channels of mostly rubbish, gaming consoles were still yet to hit their stride, people stayed away from football for fear of their own life, the internet wasn't a thing that existed in the world of any but the most techy of geeks, and smartphones were not yet even a twinkle in the milkman's eye. So basically you go to the pub and watch a band, or you stay home and play Connect 4. Well, perhaps not, but you get my drift. There were plenty of towns in the nearby vicinity with a pub that would give you a gig if you were able to produce even the most utilitarian of demo tapes, coupled with a badly photocopied and badly written biography

- perhaps including a bad photograph if you were particularly keen. It might be a support slot on a Tuesday night, but beggars can't be choosers and support slots on a Tuesday night are a far more sensible way to learn your craft than headlining on a Saturday night. A couple of things that were major contributing factors to making things a little easier... firstly, you could reach the booker of the venue via a landline[41], making it much more difficult for them to ignore you. Secondly, you could generally turn up to the pub in question when there were bands on and meet them face to face, an option that seems to have stopped being an option in most cases many years ago now. One thing that has remained steady has been the fees paid to bands at these sort of gigs, which was bugger all back then and is bugger all now. My first band did fifteen shows, and I kept a record of how much we got paid. We averaged a mighty £8.46 per show, although this was weighted rather unfairly by the time someone actually paid us a massive £60 for a show – admittedly only because the main act had dropped out, meaning we had to be support and headliner, something of a tricky call for a band that only knew nine songs.

As the internet and mobile phone era kicked off, booking a gig became much easier in theory, yet much harder in practice. You can send out an email with ease but - presuming you've made it past the spam filter, and presuming the email address still works, and presuming the booker actually checks their email, and presuming that once checking it they don't simply delete yours - you still need to grab their attention and hope that they check out the links you've

---

41   Which, for younger viewers, are the sort of telephones your grandparents had, phones that were always fully charged and always conveniently placed somewhere in the house so that everyone else within the house had no choice but to listen to your conversation.

sent them and fancy giving you a spot. Over a period of a year myself and a friend, who ran another band, monitored the success rate of emailing bookers and venues and worked out that we were getting a response from one in seventeen emails, and when the response came there was about a one in three chance of getting a show. So on average fifty-one emails to get a show. Mobile phones *did* make things easier for a while, but then bookers realised that it was easier to just not have voicemail and to ignore calls at any time other than between 9.45am and 10.05am on every second Tuesday of alternate months. Thing is, you don't *expect* to get a gig from every venue you contact, you know you'll have mixed success and that is completely fine. It's the not knowing that kills you. If you send out twenty emails and get one reply offering a show and nineteen replies saying thanks but no thanks then that would be great. Really great! You can scratch them off the list and move on. But you almost never get a rejection. Did they get the email? Did they read it? Better follow up with another email. Still no reply. Am I pissing them off now? Do they just not like us? Are there no slots available right now? Is my email domain blacklisted? Should we try again in a few months? Do I need a new email address? Who knows? In an attempt to make things as easy as possible for the booker, I came up with a method that worked quite well and got a record number of responses. Before I launched into the usual spiel of introducing the band and providing some links to our work, I would begin the email as follows:

> *Hi! We're looking for a gig – you can find out all about the band below. We know you're busy, but we'd really appreciate a response to this email even if you don't have a show for us, so we can stop pestering you in future - simply type the number 1, 2, 3 or 4 as your reply.*

1. *Yes, we'd like to give you a date – please get back to us for options*
2. *Sorry, we're fully booked at present, try again in six months*
3. *Sorry, your band isn't really right for our venue*
4. *Your band is shit, please don't ever contact us again*

Curiously, nobody ever replied with just the number as asked, but I'd get a number of responses along the lines of *"lol, nice one, nothing right now but try again at the end of the month"*. I didn't get any more gigs than usual, but the response rate tripled, so I'm putting that down as a win.

Once you are actually lucky enough to strike up a conversation with a booker, you'll get offered a possible date, or perhaps if you're lucky a couple of different dates to choose from. Generally the rule of thumb is the more you want the gig, the less likely you are to be able to do it. And inevitably you're not entirely sure you can do it without checking with the rest of the band, so you must go through the rigmarole of getting hold of the booker again, to give them your answer. It's not realistic to ask your band members to keep every night free for the foreseeable future, especially when it's to do something that may well lose them money, or in the best-case scenario make them not very much money. But that's pretty much what is required, at least if you're in any way serious. I had an integral member of a band that would never play a show on New Year's Eve as that was for family, which, you know, is fine and all that, but you're a musician and New Year's Eve gigs are the best paying shows - I had to turn down fantastic earners three years running because of this. Booking a tour is harder still – while your bandmates have agreed to be available over a set period, you then have to line up all the venues in a convenient window. Getting a gig in areas you've not been to before can be tough, especially if it's overseas, so like a pothead in Amsterdam, you eagerly grab at pretty much anything that's offered. This is why you end up playing in London on Thursday, Glasgow on Friday and then Oxford on Saturday.

A valuable tip I should pass on here is to never ever bloody well *ever* cc members of your band into emails to bookers. Especially do not do this if you have a band member who is perhaps prone to angry sweary outbursts towards an industry that has not always been good to him and who carries not so much a chip as a whole bag of potatoes on his shoulder as a result. On the positive side, if you do make this mistake, as I did, you will only make it once. We had a venue cancel a gig on us via email at just a few days' notice, as they'd double booked us – I copied in my band members in the reply to them, so that they all knew what was going on, stating firmly but professionally that this was not good enough – we'd paid for radio advertising for this show, and stood to be down several hundred dollars as a result, so are we going to be compensated accordingly? This resulted in angry sweary band member replying to me that he knew the booker in question, and he was a "goddam fucking arsehole with shit for brains" who was not the sort of person we should be dealing with anyway and it would perhaps be for the best if he died a horrible death. Luckily this reply, meant for my eyes only, was sent using the rightly much maligned "reply to all" function, so not only had I got it, but so did the booker. ARGH. I went into a massive damage control exercise worthy of a team of Tory spin doctors, and I ended up concluding the episode on surprisingly good terms with the booker in question – personally. But there was no way in hell we were getting another gig at his sadly rather good venue. You can do a brilliant gig at a venue and be a pleasure to deal with, and the booker will perhaps tell a few friends good things about your band and a bit of progress will be made. Or you can do something like this, and – apology or not, and despite the fact that the venue caused us a massive problem and cost us good money in the first place – you can absolutely guarantee that the booker will be telling all and sundry to avoid your arsehole band at all costs. Under the circumstances it's hard to argue with this too.

This doesn't mean that you don't have the absolute right to get thoroughly pissed off with bookers, and you will. You hear some right old bollocks sometimes that just make no sense at all. I was once trying to organise a show at a cracking venue in our hometown as the centrepiece of an album launch tour. I was in dialogue for months with the booker, who had expressed how he was always keen to help local independent bands and how he was really impressed with what we were doing. The problem arose when I started trying to actually nail down a date. It was part of a sixteen-date tour spread over a month, and naturally you need these things planned out well in advance so that you can plan and promote accordingly. After months of being offered promises of a date without actually *getting* a date, I made a final attempt to nail it down. Only to be told that I can't have a date any more than four weeks in advance. Why can't I book three months in advance? *We can only offer four weeks*. But there are other gigs on your website up to nine months in advance! *Yes, but they're touring bands.* Well we're a touring band too – I'm literally booking a tour here! *Yes, but you're local, we reserve dates beyond a month in advance for international or interstate acts*. So you're not prepared to help local acts? *Yes, I'll give you a date, but you'll have to wait until nearer the time.* But I'm booking a whole tour, what if the dates aren't available in a few months' time because you've given them to non-local bands? *Nah, you should be ok.* Oh, well if it *should* be ok then I'll just go and plan everything on that basis shall I? In retrospect, perhaps this was the email chain I should have cc'd the band in on[42].

I have thus far been calling bookers "bookers", although the term is interchangeable with "promoters". I can't bring myself to call them promoters though, as this term implies that they actually promote something, so I've stuck with booker. Which isn't to say there aren't a number of bookers that actually deserve the title promoter. Many venues – and for some mysterious reason these tend to be the venues that always have a crowd, a good reputation, and stay in business year in year out – actually promote their own shows. Others think this is an absurd idea and that the only promotion should be done by the band, presumably because all bands are absolute experts at marketing, with generous budgets to boot. The best venues will book good bands on a bill with another band or two that are mutually compatible, that are likely to appeal to a similar crowd, and they'll have some degree of quality control. They will often have no admission charge. They will play suitable and varied music between acts. This approach gains a venue a good reputation, thus the crowds will start going to the venue because they generally have good bands, and if they don't like the band well hey, they didn't pay to get in anyway. The venue provides an inhouse sound engineer, and pays the band a set fee, and they can do this because people are coming in the door and drinking because

---

[42] Never ever bloody well *ever* cc members of your band into emails to bookers.

they know the music will be good.

Another approach that many other venues take – which, for some ineffable reason, is never anything like as successful - is to offer dates to a band and request they supply the rest of the bands too, or to perhaps put a bill together based on the order of the emails in their inbox, rather than an outdated concept such as musical compatibility. The band can book their own sound engineer, although for twice as much as the going rate the venue will supply one themselves[43]. And hey, why not get the band to provide their own door bitch[44] to stamp people's hands on entry and take their money, every band has a friend who'd be delighted to do that yeah? And as the band are paying for someone to do this and doing all the work it seems only fair that the venue take a fifty percent cut of the door takings. These venues also take a very specific, highly targeted approach to advertising, which is to write the names of the bands playing that night on a blackboard by the door when they open up, thereby ensuring that everyone who enters the venue to see your band can see that your band is indeed playing. They supercharge this approach by putting one of the twelve posters you sent them a month ago up behind the bar on the night before the gig. We sound-checked at one such fine establishment and then, with one hour to go before we hit the stage, watched the venue put up our posters that we'd personally dropped off six weeks prior. We then got moaned at after the show for not bringing enough people. You know these gigs are shit, but you still end up doing them – it may be all that is on offer, and the venues, though rarely

---

43 i.e. give you the number of their mate and leave it to you to organise. The soundman will then turn up ten minutes before you go on stage, and piss off to the bar five minutes after you start.

44 The term door bitch applies regardless of the sex of said bitch. I don't find it a particularly pleasant term, but it's not my doing!

successful and long-lived, have a never-ending queue of desperate young bands ready to give it a shot. And the thing about desperate young bands is they don't demand any money and they still have plenty of mates ready to go out for a night of music and drinking at the drop of a hat. I've done plenty of great shows at this sort of place, but there's no money in it. Let's say fifty people (optimistic, but keeps the maths simple) come in and pay $10 each, that's $500. Take away $200 as the venue's door cut, then $150 for the soundman, then $50 to the door bitch. That leaves you with $100 to split between the three bands – nice work if you can get it eh? Even if you filled the pub with a hundred payers that's only $400 between the three bands, and if you've brought in a hundred payers then you've probably done some paid advertising such as an ad in the local music press which cost you $180, plus a decent run of posters for say $50. So if each band has four members, selling out the venue has made each musician just over $14 each. Before petrol. And yet… the venue make their money, the sound engineer gets paid, the booker gets paid, security get paid, the bar staff get paid… so while the band earns next to nothing, it is also the crucial component of an industry that employees a vast number of people, many of whom wouldn't have work if it wasn't for the bands themselves. I find it's best not to dwell on that.

If you want to play gigs, then writing a biography for your band is one hundred percent unavoidable, a necessary evil that will blight your entire career unless you get to the stage when someone else will be paid to do all this stuff for you. It's definitely one of the worst things about getting gigs, although I'm undecided as yet as to whether it's worse or better than dealing with the actual bookers themselves. This is a bit of a choose-the-tastiest-turd contest though – there are no real winners. In the early days it is especially difficult to write a bio, as your band has no history and no story to tell. We, and I suspect most others, got around this by simply making stuff up. After a while we decided to just invent odd and irrelevant stories instead, stuff that had little or nothing to do with the band but was marginally more readable than "The band are from Basingstoke and formed last year, their favourite bands are The Smiths and The Fall. Singer Shaun is 18, and sounds a little like Robert Smith". Nobody cares. Nobody reads them. It's just something you have to do to show willing. If your band is doing anything of note then most bookers have probably heard of you anyway. The biography has become partly redundant in the internet era, as it's much easier just to give somebody your website address and be done. But then you start applying for festivals. Oh. Dear. God.

On most levels the festival gigs are a step up on the average pub and club shows. In the last ten years or so I've lost count of how many I've played at, but the figure is probably at least thirty times less than the number I've *applied* to play at. At the upper end of the scale bands are actually invited to play at these festivals, but for the mere mortals among us there will be an application process. For most festivals nowadays there's usually a fairly slick web-based form to complete, with perhaps a few uploads to add, such as a photo or an mp3 file. They'll also provide a drop-down box where you can select the musical genre that most suits your band, which for some reason only contains genres that your band definitely isn't. Occasionally I still come across the odd little festival that will ask you to print out a form, fill it in by hand and post it along with a CD, which seems really quite quaint nowadays.

Amongst a plethora of requested information, three things that they will *always* want on these applications are:

1. A one sentence description of your act

2. A longer biography

3. A photo

Well that's not a big ask really is it? Yes. Yes it bloody is. I mean, in theory all you have to do is write a cheesy sentence such as "Bastard Death Squad are a 4-piece jazz metal band setting fire to dancefloors all over the world" or some other bollocks, and a longer biography perhaps mentioning something about your new album, where you've toured, members of the band, or who you sound a bit like. Easy enough – write these once, and then it's copy and paste all the way baby. Except, that is, for one major stumbling block...

I'm not sure, but I think what happens is that there is some sort of national committee meeting at the start of every year between people that organise festivals. At these meetings they all draw lots to decide who will request what on their application forms, and there is to be no doubling up whatsoever. What this means is that when you're asked for a one sentence summary of your act, the first application will state *"please provide a one sentence summary of your act in 20 words"*. The next application will state *"please provide a one sentence summary of your act in 40-50 words"*. The next will state *"please provide a once sentence summary of your act in 100 characters or less"*. The next will state *"please provide a one sentence summary of your act in no more than 10 words"*. Some will add in qualifiers such as *"make sure you mention your latest release"* or *"be sure to include your dietary requirements"*. And so it goes on, meaning that for every application you make you need to rewrite your bloody sentence. I have a word document for one of my previous bands which has thirty-two variants of essentially the same sentence, and being able to simply copy and paste a past sentence is a rare treat indeed. The same holds true for item two, the full biography. *100 words, 200 words, 500 words, 842-character limit, please include details of band members, please summarise all your previous accomplishments, be sure to mention bands that you sound like, please don't include details of band members, list any and all pets etc etc.* It is, frankly, cruel. The bio is a horrible thing to write full stop, and making you constantly rewrite it is borderline mental abuse. Part of the whole biography hell thing is having to describe what your band sounds like, presumably for people too time-impoverished and musically dyslexic to spend thirty seconds listening to you and working it out for themselves – although to be fair this is sometimes so they can publish it in the festival program or on their website[45]. One issue here is that your band probably sounds nothing like what you think it sounds like – a common factor in this being that bands have a tendency to mix up "sounds like" with "influenced by". Sure, you might have been inspired by the likes of Scott Walker, Lou Reed and Jimi Hendrix, but that really doesn't help matters when you sound like James Blunt. Musicians are awful judges of what their band sounds like, but then so are the audience, so it's a most vexing issue. In the end I reckon the safest best is to choose three or four acts that you're happy to associate with:

---

[45] Yes, not only do you have to provide the bio, but you have to do so knowing that thousands of other people may well read it, and make a judgement on you accordingly. I'd frequently get a festival program on arrival at a festival, and cringe as I saw my hopeless attempt to summarise the band in print. For a while this would really get to me, but one day I sat down and read everyone's little promo spiel and realised that with almost no exceptions they were all equally awful, which was really nice.

1. A legendary act that everyone has heard of.

2. A popular contemporary band that has some street cred.

3. A band that nobody but you has ever heard of.

4. A group that sound nothing like you whatsoever, but that people like.

Which leaves the photo from our original list, but again this is never simply a photo, the qualifiers are here too – *must be 300dpi, must be 450 x 300 pixels, must be 72dpi, must be at least 1000 x 600 pixels, must be no more than 1mb in size, must be square*. So you end up with eighteen copies of the same picture on your hard drive, all badly labelled so that you can have the joy of opening them all each time you need one so you can see which one is which.

One more note on the dreaded biography – I recently saw a tweet from an author making much the same points as I've made here, and I took some solace in the discovery that at least it wasn't a torture especially reserved for bands!

In my early days, getting a gig in London was a real accomplishment. After all, that's where all the cool people were, and all the A&R folk too[46]. Of course London is a big place and a broad term, and there was a world of difference between a show at Dingwalls in Camden Town

---

[46] Well, the one A&R person (Artist & Repertoire – basically a talent spotter) in the country that still actually went to gigs anyway.

and a show at the Dog & Duck in Acton, but you can still write London in your press release[47]. Bookers in London knew they were the cool people with the most sought-after gigs, so were always exponentially harder to get hold of, possibly because they spent a large amount of time up their own arses[48]. Once you'd got hold of them on your twenty third phone call and managed to get a prime slot at 11.15pm on a Monday night, you could start to calculate exactly how much the gig would cost you. A very common part of the deal with these shows, for bands from outside London, was that you would bring a coach full of your own fans to the gig. This was not something you could really blag either – I recall many a venue that stipulated that a contract between you and the coach company be supplied well in advance, or no gig. The venue would then supply you with tickets that you could sell and thus earn your own fee, by which I mean sell nearly enough to pay for the coach hire if you were exceptionally lucky. And selling tickets for the Monday night gig/coach trip to your local fans and friends who can see you play on a regular basis on a weekend for next to nothing is not the easiest sell at the best of times. There's a risk factor involved too – we did one of these shows in London and had a coach load of people coming along. We arrived at the venue to find it had closed down the previous week. Which was awkward. There's no fun like the hanging-around-on-the-street-outside-a-boarded-up-pub-for-two-hours-on-a-November-evening-waiting-for-a-coach-load-of-people-to-turn-up-so-that-you-can-tell-them-to-go-home kind of fun.

---

47 Nobody will read it, but you will feel better, which is important.
48 I once presumed that you couldn't get any further up your own arse than a London band booker, but that was before I'd encountered Melbourne.

Getting a residency at a venue is a tricky call. They're notoriously difficult to get, but they are a brilliant way to build an audience. We did a four-week run of Wednesday nights and the first one had about twelve people there, but the crowd grew every week as word got around and the last show was packed. You can make decent money this way too[49], and instead of advertising one gig at a time you can advertise all four together! The last time I got a residency was when I'd approached a venue near my bass player Steve's house, having seen that they had regular residencies happening, and got nowhere. But Steve then went to the venue with me one night, and it turned out he was friends with the manager, and we were duly offered an eight week(!) run[50]. This was a surprise - Steve was usually a little hopeless to be honest, and rarely bothered to turn up to rehearsal, even the ones that were arranged to take place at his house. He also turned up to gigs when he felt like, rather than when the gig started, so for the first three shows of this residency we had to start playing with no bass player, which was... embarrassing. Steve called me after this and told me it wasn't all working out with the venue and the manager (his mate) had decided to cancel the rest of the shows. I could totally understand the manager's point of view here, after all we were a band with an optional bass player who didn't even seem to really know the songs when he actually did turn up. Anyway, I walked past the venue the next week and who should be playing bass for the band there that night but Steve. Hmm. Some weeks later I sauntered past again, and bumped into the manager...

"Hey man, what happened to you guys, you just disappeared!"

"No... you sacked us, remember?"

---

[49] This is why residencies tend to go to bands that are good mates of the booker.
[50] See previous footnote.

"Eh? What? I loved you guys!"

"Steve told me you had fired us!"

"What? He told me you'd had enough - I had to book his other band to replace you at short notice... oh."

Bookers can be awful, but sometimes not nearly as awful as band members.

While residencies are nice, a casual regular gig at a venue is nearly as good. If you play a good show with a decent crowd, you might be lucky enough to negotiate another date there and then, although more often than not the person you need to impress - and then organise a date with - is not there. So they haven't see you play, and haven't seen the crowd. And while the bar manager or the soundman may lavish you with praise, it's of very little practical use when it comes to repeat bookings. Many venues simply sub-contract the bookings out to someone who rarely steps foot in the venue. But when the booker is in attendance, one decent gig can lead to them pencilling you in for a show every six weeks or so for the next year, which is rather lovely. I once did eight shows over the course of a year in this manner at one venue, and it's wonderful to be given a whole bunch of dates without going through all the usual nonsense that it normally takes to get just one. That said, sometimes it doesn't matter how good you are or how many people come through the door. Exhibit A: we played a show in Melbourne which just went off – a packed house that we kept dancing all night, a brilliant reaction, and a small fortune in door money that the venue got a very tasty cut from. We literally couldn't have done any better. Now, the booker was in attendance that night, and as luck would have it was in fact being the door bitch for the night – e.g. watching exactly how many people came in, taking their money, and seeing the band blow the roof off the place. Well at least we'll be guaranteed another show here I thought, naively. So when the place had emptied out at the end of the night, I approached the booker and asked if we could get another date in a couple of months' time. The answer, I shit you not, was *"Well, send me your demo and I'll have a think about it"*. We never played there again.

When my band started getting regular work on the festival circuit, I became aware of the notion of insurance for bands, more specifically public liability insurance. Despite playing hundreds of shows over the previous couple of decades, I'd never been asked to provide any insurance. Then, all of a sudden, it became A Thing. As far as I could tell at the time, some bright spark[51] worked out that instead of their festival taking out an all-encompassing insurance policy, they could save a small fortune by putting the onus onto the bands to provide their own public liability insurance. Initially this was just the big festivals doing it, but within a couple of years every tin pot festival was asking for a certificate of insurance to be provided along with the band's application to play at the event. I've still yet to meet a musician that's actually had cause to claim on this insurance. Even the most wild and hedonistic bands I've been in or known have stopped well short of causing injury to the general public that might necessitate recourse to legal compensation. I can see why it might be required for a massive stadium rock tour by Kiss, complete with assorted props and pyrotechnics, but it's hard to envisage a likely scenario whereby your average folk festival act is causing serious injury to the punters.

---

51 Or to put it another way, some complete and utter bastard.

There were a couple of years when we had to buy insurance at a cost of about seven hundred dollars just to do a couple of festivals at which we made distinctly less than about seven hundred dollars in profit. There was one particularly lean year financially speaking when we simply couldn't afford the insurance and, well, let's just say it's times like these when you really begin to appreciate the photoshop skills you've developed over the years.

Ultimately most bands take any gig they're offered as they're physically incapable of turning them down, which seems very unfair on the bands. This is in part due to the difficulty of getting the damn things, and in part due to the eternal optimism that any show *might* just turn out to be really bloody good. You never know if the next show at the Horse and Jockey in Craptown is going to be the one where you finally meet the person who loves your band, has unlimited cash resources, and will manage you all the way to the big time[52].

---

[52] Well, you do know, but you're in denial.

7.
THE MANAGER

As you now know from the previous chapter, booking gigs is a bloody nightmare, and a hugely time-consuming business. Of course, from a fairly young age you're aware of the concept of managers and the notion that they do all this sort of stuff for you, for a share of the money. Accordingly, the prospect of getting one becomes something of a major target to a young band, an answer to all your prayers, and the missing ingredient in the package that will fast track you to fame and fortune once obtained. I'm not sure whether that is still the case, as I gave up on the notion of having one about ten years ago, after a particularly woeful experience, and resigned myself to doing everything myself forever more in the knowledge that I'd been doing it for so long by this time that I may as well keep doing so. And like every other creative industry in the twenty first century there is bugger all money in it for the most part, so managing yourself becomes the only choice most people have.

In the early days, when you are young and not eaten up inside by the cynicism that experience inevitably brings to all but the most positive or successful musicians, you tend to get numerous vague offers of management from all sorts of people. All sorts of people who aren't managers. It goes like this... from your late teens to perhaps your mid-twenties, you tend to have far more friends than you'll have as you get older. You're all going out to pubs, clubs and gigs week-in week-out, meeting new people, getting drunk with them and effectively doing some good networking as a by-product of this. Your mates actually turn up to see your band, as it's still something of a novelty, and there is a certain coolness by association to be had for some people in doing this. Of course, when they're older, you'll find it easier to get them to come to a street protest campaigning for the cruel torture and genocide of little fluffy kittens than to one of your gigs, but for the moment they're there on a regular basis. Mates see shows played to decent sized and enthusiastic crowds, get caught up in the excitement, and the idea takes hold that perhaps they could be involved in some way. There are two options for this really – ask the band if you can help out as a roadie, which seems to involve a little too much heavy lifting, or offer to manage them, which seems a little more sedate and possibly a little more glamorous. None of these people have the faintest idea what this involves of course, but how hard can it be, right? They already know that being in a band isn't a real job. I have had two hundred and thirty-six post-gig conversations with acquaintances who have expressed an interest in managing the band, full of enthusiasm at the prospect of being involved - of which precisely zero have resulted in any form of management subsequently occurring. I don't blame them for this in the slightest, but I have had people be genuinely offended by my lack of enthusiasm towards their offers. It doesn't take long to work out that there is no money to be made. Being a musician is one of the most effective ways of getting rid of money that's ever been invented, rivalled only by getting a massive cocaine or gambling habit. Even the most naïve individual soon works out that ten or twenty percent of not very much money is not very much money, and that, barring major commercial success, you're on a hiding to nothing. Which is absolutely fine. Musicians do it because we have to, not for the financial rewards, and we simply don't know how to stop. We're probably missing a crucial gene or something. More well-balanced rational thinkers stay well away, and they are entirely sensible to do so.

None of which means that bands don't still yearn for a proper manager, and in fairness this is only partially motivated by laziness. The main motivation is to have someone who knows what they're doing look after promoting your band, booking better gigs with their army of contacts, and approach record companies with their professional charm. I mean I'm pretty sure Coca-Cola aren't getting the guy who mixes up the syrup at the factory to do their marketing, Google aren't letting the people who code their algorithms anywhere near their sales department, and musicians should likewise not be allowed to manage their bands. Oh well.

I'm sure there is such a thing as a really good manager, and I'm sure many bands have them[53]. I've never met one myself, but I've encountered a whole bunch of managers – some nice, some arseholes, but all ultimately pretty bloody hopeless to varying degrees. The first one that showed an interest in one of my bands was a dude called Oni. Or was it Odi? Omi? Ori? Something short that started with O anyway. We'd played an absolutely brilliant hometown gig one Saturday night, selling out a 700+ capacity venue that just went

---

[53] Although a huge percentage of horror stories in this industry seem to relate to managers who steal all the cash from their artists and ride off into the sunset.

crazy. It still ranks as one of my most memorable gigs to this day. The singer, Robbie, got a call the next morning at seven in the bloody AM from this guy, I mean really, who wants a phone call at that time on a Sunday morning? Nobody, that's who. Even if I've just won the lottery I'd rather wait until a decent hour to find out, and that's without factoring in the gig that we got back from about four hours earlier. Nevertheless, Robbie was awakened from his slumber and Oni introduced himself as a manager. His daughter had been at the gig – she'd introduced herself to us and got Robbie's number - and told her Dad to get straight onto us as we were apparently the best band she'd ever seen and notably better than any of his other acts. So he did, and on the basis of his daughter's recommendation he said he wanted to meet us straight away and manage us, promising the world to us from the start. Naturally an excited Robbie phoned me immediately to relay this information, deciding on balance that if he had been woken up at such an ungodly hour then it was only fair that I was as well. A meeting in a pub ensued soon after, and noises were made that he had a producer who had just worked on the latest album by The Verve (Urban Hymns, that was just breaking in a major way at the time) with whom he'd love to get us working. This was all very exciting, and he kept telling us how much he trusted his daughter's judgement that we were something special. We had no gigs in the immediate future, so he came along to see us rehearse, at which point we began to suspect that he was, in fact, a bit of a dick, and didn't actually trust his daughter's judgement one bit. After listening to a few songs he began suggesting we change a few of the arrangements and sounds, and – major red flag - maybe some of the lyrics, suggestions met with very short shrift by us. He also dangled the possibility of getting us in the studio with David Bowie and doing one of the songs with him as a duet, and the bullshit detectors all exploded at once. Later in the week he said he thought we were ok (gee thanks!) but what he wanted was a tape of all our songs with just a vocal and acoustic guitar so that he could get his producer to work out some new arrangements and sounds for us. Dude, just stick us in the studio, we got this. In the meantime I heard some stuff by the main act he represented, leading me to further question his judgement vis-à-vis not having any. I remember telling Robbie to tell Oni to fuck right off – Robbie took the middle ground and did a tape of some of the songs with just vocal and guitar, and then gave up and added a verbal postscript to the tape stating that this was a stupid idea and we never heard from him again. Oh well.

I remember one guy who was ok, got us a few good gigs and was generally helpful for a brief period, but then like so many others decided he could start having some creative input into the songs. This is a sure-fire way to end any artist-manager relationship. Remember that therapist in Metallica's Some Kind of Monster documentary? It's a line you just can't cross. Besides which, this manager was already causing some unexpected problems. Sure, he had a van that he was happy to drive us into London with for gigs, but it was an unmarked white van and he had a thick Irish accent. And around this time, London was experiencing a wave of terrorist bombings, and thirty-something year old tough looking Irish guys driving unmarked white vans are pretty bloody high on the list of people who machine-gun-wielding armoured police officers like to stop and thoroughly search when they're driving into London. Making it very tricky to get to gigs in a timely manner, and not exactly creating a relaxed stress-free state of mind for one's performance. Oh well.

The best manager I ever had was a bloke called Daryl. I say best because I actually got something useful out of him (weed). As an actual manager he turned out to be comically awful. The problem is that as a band you're so keen to have someone help you out that it's easy to fall for the charm of people who turn out to be as useful as a chocolate fireplace. We did a rip-roaring show in rural Australia, which is no mean feat for any band that isn't playing the peculiarly unique brand of Aussie pub rock so loved there. Daryl approached us after the gig and said he wanted to manage us – he had a management company that booked shows all over the country, mainly in the rural areas (outside of a few massive cities, Australia is populated rather sparsely by any number of small towns, and the country is so big that they're all in the middle of nowhere). These shows are not exactly glamorous, but they tend to pay ok as many bands simply have no interest in doing them - and they can be great fun. Sometimes it feels like the whole town has come out for the night. Which often they have. They're also not easy to get without good contacts, so a manager who can get you these shows is a useful addition. We arranged to meet up and Daryl won over any initial scepticism by giving me a large bag of weed for free. Promises were made, a deal was struck, and things looked to have potential. I think he was taking twenty percent of all our performance fees, which was twenty percent of gigs we wouldn't be playing otherwise, so it seemed an acceptable deal. We did a few shows around the state, and his partner came along and watched us at one of them. We chatted and all was good, and then the next morning I received a lengthy and unintentionally hilarious email detailing all of the ways we had gone wrong at the show – not least of which was our poor choice of clothing, which was categorically NOT what we were wearing on the poster, which had apparently upset the landlord considerably. In fact it was looking distinctly possible that if I wasn't careful I may well end up in detention. It seemed rather strange though, to berate us for not bringing the energy of our full band show to a three hour acoustic performance on the patio of a pub on a Sunday lunchtime, and the scolding was even more strange given that we were received well by a crowd that enthusiastically spent their money on our merchandise. This all led to a crisis meeting at which once again a large bag of weed was donated to me on arrival, and Spider and I sat their getting stoned while pretending to listen to Daryl's grievances against us. Promises were made of thousands of dollars to be invested in the recording of a new album and there was talk of getting us to play Glastonbury as Daryl was a good friend of Michael Eavis, the proprietor of said festival. It was hard to reconcile this level of industry contacts with the guy in front of us who complained about the gig posters we'd supplied him and replaced them with designs of his own - which were basically all your worst colour and font nightmares combined into one and filtered through Microsoft Paint at the wrong resolution. I mean, *he actually used the Comic Sans font*. Telling him so didn't endear us to him any further. But we kept things amicable because hey, thousands of dollars were still being dangled. And then another meeting occurred where we played Daryl some demos of new songs we had lined up and, inevitably, out came the song-writing advice and creative instructions, including the always well-received suggestions for changes to lyrics. Up until this point I had never considered that there was some bullshit simply not worth putting up with, even in exchange for free weed, but it turns out I was very much wrong, and that was the end of that. Well, not quite the end, as Daryl then claimed that we owed him for the weed he'd "given" us. Yeah... good luck with that. We honoured a few remaining gigs, but we'd been foolish enough to pass some of our own contacts to him so he could book up more shows for us, saving us the trouble. Chasing these up ourselves later we realised that he'd been pretty enthusiastic about doing just that, leading to several conversations with said contacts where we attempted to undo the damage done - *"who was that guy, we thought he was winding us up and just ignored him, sorry!"*.

The phrase we'd continually come back to with managers was "show me the money!", which is probably a very sensible approach to take, even if it does have the major downside of making you think of Tom Cruise. Great. Now I'm thinking about Tom Cruise. If you're going to talk yourself up and tell us how great you're going to be for the band, then prove it. Invest. Money talks, much louder than promises. And if the manager has no other successful bands that they're working with, then perhaps take that as enlightening evidence of their managerial abilities.

8.
THE RECORD COMPANY

The holy grail for most bands is to score themselves a record deal. To a young band this seems to be the main thing you need to achieve in your quest for success. Although as you get older you realise there's a lot more to it than that - once you get yourself a deal, the battle is only just beginning. A lot of bands that get signed up (I suspect the majority) never go on to any further success, although that does rather depend on your definition of success, and are dropped fairly quickly. I've had a number of friends that have signed deals, and very exciting it was too for all concerned, but not one of them progressed any further as a result, and in every instance their band ended up splitting when the record label dropped them after their first one or two releases. Some of them racked up sizeable debts in the process.

I've had precious few dealings with record companies myself. The nearest I got was a couple of distribution deals, which basically involved a label taking on the distribution of an album. In theory, the label would try to sell my album, get it into stores, and handle the stuff I wasn't really able to do myself, for a cut of the profits. There was no investment in the band as such, but they were prepared to push the product, which was better than a kick in the teeth. However, with no money being injected for marketing this was a hiding to nothing.

I have on many occasions done what most bands do, and sent off numerous CDs to as many record labels as I could find, in the hope of finding that holy grail, but of course I never did. I got the traditional rejection letter a good few times – credit to most record companies, they seem to usually have a pretty polite and efficient rejection process in place! Eventually I just gave up and simply released everything independently, working on the accurate assumption that record companies will be breaking down your door if you can create a buzz and shift some records off your own back, so worry about it when it happens.

But there was one memorable instance when I was asked to come into a meeting with a record company in Melbourne, on the basis of one of my demo CD submissions. I was pretty excited about this. Picture the scene – it's Monday and I've been driving back from some weekend gigs in the country, and just have time to nip home and change before heading off to the meeting. I arrive home, change my shirt and grab the only clean pair of trousers I can find, some tatty but groovy and comfortable old jeans. It's a stinking hot summer day, so I make what will soon become a regrettable decision to go without underwear. Arriving just about in time for the meeting, I'm introduced to a very likeable and business-like young woman who works for the label. I briefly wondered that perhaps I'd heard something tear as I slumped down in the chair opposite her desk, but thought nothing of it and we chatted for about ten minutes - but she seemed very distracted and the conversation was a little awkward.

The meeting finished quite abruptly with her telling me she had to rush off somewhere, and heading straight out of her office before I even had time to stand up. Somewhat nonplussed by what had just happened, I looked down and realised that the tearing sound I had heard was in fact my jeans. Tearing at the groin. Now, you'll recall at this point that I had opted to go underwear-free for the afternoon. Which of course meant that I had been sitting opposite her with everything very much hanging out, on a very much unavoidable display. I didn't hear any more from her, and I decided that perhaps in this instance I wouldn't chase her up to find out why. If by some slim chance she ever reads this, I would like to take this opportunity to say that I really am so very, very sorry.

9.
IN THE STUDIO

There are very few things for a young band that seem as exciting as going into the studio to record your masterpiece – and very few things in life where the reality is so wildly removed from the imagination. The rush of excitement when you enter the studio, see the enormous mixing desk, admire rack after rack of gadgets with lots of LED lights on them and weird names like Gain Spanker or Flangulation Giblifier (that do stuff you don't understand, and quite probably never will), and set up all your gear in a proper acoustically treated space... well, it soon disappears. Usually at some point in the third hour of the first day, when you've done nothing but drink tea and listen to the engineer and the drummer spend the whole morning trying to remove the ringing sound from the second rack tom. Much later in the process the drummer will of course tell you that the second rack tom is hit once, near the end of the weakest song of the three you are recording.

I've always had a fascination for recording music ever since I first picked up a guitar. I've recorded hundreds of songs in many studios and I really enjoy it, but it can be a very expensive habit. I had a friend with whom I used to do bootleg recordings of gigs, which back in the late eighties generally meant recording a gig with a crap handheld tape recorder (which was the style at the time). Now to take the ferry cost a nickel, so you'd smuggle the tape recorder into the venue, record the gig whilst trying to keep the mic in a sensible place that isn't your pocket but is still hidden from security, yet still drink beer and enjoy yourself. Then the next day make some copies with your twin cassette deck with dual auto direction capability, and create some black and white cassette inlays to photocopy on to some coloured paper – more often than not a golden yellow colour. People would sell them for a quid at Camden Market, a local independent record shop, or from a suitcase outside a gig, like a musical Derek Trotter. I must have bought about thirty of these things, and they were – like the one's I made myself – almost irredeemably shit. But they were kinda cool too. Back then in pre-YouTube days, unless you actually saw a band, you weren't going to hear what they were playing on tour. As a fan I loved them, but I suspect the bands hated them – much like I hate seeing a crappy video of my band filmed on someone's phone and uploaded to YouTube. But it was a valuable way of getting a sneak preview of new material at times, even though it was often like hearing a new song from two doors down the road interspersed with occasional loud voice-over commentary from drunken bystanders – "sorry mate can I squeeze through?", "fucks sake, careful", "mind the beer man". I had a bootleg of Zodiac Mindwarp & the Love Reaction playing at the Marquee in London's Charing Cross Road, and for a few songs you can hear a dude loudly explaining that the band are crap and that he hates them. After about four songs another voice interrupts the brutal critiquing with the harsh but fair request that the owner of the first voice shut the fuck up else his fucking teeth will be all over the fucking floor you fucking cunt. Anyway, I've sort of forgotten the point of this digression. It may well have been that I was making crap recordings from an early age.

I used to hold an unshakeable belief that I could reasonably expect a cheap version of something good to be just as good as the something good thing itself, which was of course too expensive. Learning the error of this thinking took many a long year. As well as in the musical domain, this attitude has had me in all sorts of trouble in areas as varied as purchasing a car, buying drugs, and booking flights. I refused to change my beliefs despite a steadily growing pile of evidence that my beliefs were possibly somewhat ill-advised, which I suppose is what life is like for many religious people. I applied this thinking to my first attempts at recording music.

The first thing you want to able to do is record multiple tracks. It's all very well having one microphone socket on your Dad's hi-fi, but what if you had <gasp> four? Well I enjoyed a stroll around the Tandy store in town as much as the next man, looking at all the electrical accessories, cables, adaptors and assorted gizmos. And I knew that for about fifteen quid you could get a basic mixing console. Which was simply a box with four inputs, four faders, and a stereo output. The four inputs were ambitious as I only had one microphone. But I figured I could record a guitar track, then play the cassette of that track back with a portable cassette player that was plugged into one of the four inputs - while playing along on guitar or bass through a second input and tweaking the individual levels with the faders. My keen yet inexperienced brain realised that there was, in theory, no limit to the number of overdubs and extra tracks I could add. Yes! I had made a recording studio, eat shit Abbey Road! Later it transpired that there was, after all, a limit to the number of extra tracks I could add, and that limit was two, after which the background noise interference became louder than the instruments. Despite this, my bass player and I managed to knock out two home demos in this manner and playing around with this setup taught me a surprising number of things about how not to record music.

The project that I'd begun with the above home studio began to grow, and even though there was just the two of us, I wanted to record with a full band sound. I knew someone with a home studio rather better than mine that I could hire very cheaply, but he couldn't record drums. In some ways this was not a problem as I didn't have a drummer. It was an eight-track quarter-inch tape affair, and he had equipment such as proper microphones that weren't available to buy in Tandy, even in the locked glass cabinet section. But I wanted drums.

A friend offered to program some drums for me on his drum machine. So in my bedroom at my parent's house we programmed the drums for a couple of songs and recorded them onto his four-track porta studio (basically a fancy version of the recording facility I'd made myself[54], but functional and built by competent people). I took this tape with me to my friend's studio and after a couple of evenings work had created something which, while objectively crap, was a big step up in sound quality from my own efforts. So much so that it functioned well enough to sell out its initial pressing of fifty

---

54 In the same way that Buckingham Palace is basically just a fancy version of my shed.

cassettes, and even got favourably reviewed in the local rag, woo!

By the time I was ready to record again, I had a four-piece band, including an actual human drummer, and a home studio was no longer a viable option. Note that we're talking early nineties here, and whereas now the home studio is common and can mean a really rather impressive set up, in those days a decent home studio was a rare thing. But by the same token, an affordable "proper" recording studio was still a feasible business venture, so there were plenty of options available. We ended up somewhere in North London. I can't recall where exactly, but I do remember that it was built in the archways of a railway bridge. This looks pretty cool, but the reality was that every ten minutes a train would rattle its way overhead and we'd have to stop whatever take we were in the middle of doing and start again once the train had passed. My other enduring memory of this weekend in London is taking a bottle of whisky in my bag, and discovering at the end of the first day that the bottle had leaked and everything in the bag was now highly flammable. Also, while I had no whisky, everything now very much smelt of whisky. Damn it.

Drugs and alcohol are of course not your friends when you're trying to produce decent recordings. An occasional beer or spliff can be conducive to a friendly working environment and ease the proceedings onwards, but anything beyond that is a bit of a nightmare. And the problem here is that there is so much downtime for so many band members during a recording session, thus so much boredom, that a nice long liquid lunch at the local pub can be incredibly appealing. When you're older and wiser you can schedule the appearances of the band at the studio so they really only have to be there to do their parts, and then they can go. But when you're young the recording experience is one for the whole gang, everyone wants to be there and be involved in everything that happens. Well, at least initially they do. It's not until later, as I alluded to at the start of this chapter, that various musicians realise that this is quite incredibly boring for them. Generally the rhythm section will have their parts done early on, and bassists and drummers are not exactly renowned for their creative input after this stage. I reckon a fair estimate would be that ninety percent of rhythm sections have bugger all interest in what goes on once they're done, whereas the pub is seriously appealing to all of them at this point in proceedings. Certainly more appealing than listening to take forty-three of a mandolin solo or the eighteenth attempt at nailing the vocal. This in itself is not really the problem. The problem arises when they get back from the pub and the recording session is still going strong. It is, generally, much easier to concentrate on nailing a guitar overdub without the presence of two or three drunken piss-taking bastards in the control room. In this instance a solution worth considering is providing them with a joint and then waiting half an hour at which point there's an excellent chance they'll be asleep, and you can get back to work.

After this first experience of a half-decent studio, the next couple of recording sessions I did were once more rooted firmly in the home studio category. I had a new band, a very raw and energetic punkish 3-piece, and this band was very much skint. Not because we were good for nothing work shy layabouts, but because we spent most of our money on beer, hash and amphetamines, which seemed very important at the time. Looking back I can see why, as we were in our early twenties, on the dole or working crappy jobs in a crappy town, living in a crappy flat and with about twenty quid to our names every week - after paying rent and a small fortune on those pay-as-you-go electricity cards to keep the meter running. And boy did it run, especially in winter when you could literally watch the pennies burning up minute by minute as you calculate whether you could afford a beer and a game of pool at the local pub or whether your last fiver would have to be spent later that night on another bloody electricity card from the nearest 24-hour garage. So escaping this misery with the aid of the odd substance was a welcome relief. Anyway, as I mentioned previously, I had found myself working with a chap called Brian, who had his own PA system. Not only that, he also had a four-track studio and an eight-track mixer, and plentiful good microphones. So we set up in the warehouse at work, miked up the drums through the mixing desk and into one channel, and used the other three channels for guitar, bass and vocals. We did a couple of sessions this way, and whilst undoubtedly very raw, the recordings did sound like what we sounded like. You'll often read interviews with bands bemoaning an inability to capture their live sound in the studio, and I've always thought that was a strange thing. If you remove all the effects and sound processing from the equation and simply record the band playing live in a room, in my experience you get a very close approximation to what you sound like to an audience. I think part of the problem is that bands are trying to capture what they *think* they sound like live, rather than what they *actually* sound like. I've always been in awe of the sound of some of the Neil Young & Crazy Horse albums, and how real they are, as if the band were right there in the room with you. Neil tells the story of how his producer David Briggs would come into the studio and simply bypass all of the gear and plug the mics directly into the mixing desk. I can't find the exact quote, as Neil handily omits an index from his 500 page tomb Waging Heavy Peace, and I'm not going to reread countless tales of old automobiles and electric car projects to find it, but it seems such an elegant and obvious solution to the problem of capturing a live sound.

Something that becomes apparent when you're hiring a recording studio is that so much in fact depends not on the studio itself, but on the person operating the studio. Now, unless you're pretty successful or pretty well financed, you'll not be bringing your own engineer and producer along with you. You're more than likely producing the recording yourself, which at the early stage in your career (i.e. the stage when you don't know what you're doing) effectively means telling the engineer that something sounds a) good, or b) bad. At the lower end of the market, you're generally hiring a studio and engineer as a package, and the engineer will likely be the person that owns the studio. So it doesn't matter how big the mixing desk is, how fancy the live room looks or how much expensive effects gear is on show, if the engineer is a dick or doesn't know what they're doing - or both - then you're screwed. Similarly, a decent engineer can make you sound amazing with the bare minimum of very basic equipment. But engineers are as much at the mercy of human nature as the rest of us, and I've met a good few that go through the motions knowing full well that they're going to get paid for the session regardless. Recording your first single may be the most important day or two thus far in the life of your band, but it's just another day at the office for the engineer, who after a couple of runs through the first song has worked out that your band is a bit rubbish and probably won't be back again any time soon, and no amount of studio magic they can muster will bring this recording session to anywhere beyond below average. These engineers are basically button pushers, there to plug a few mics in, to press record and stop, and to generally contribute the bare minimum to your recording session. In fact, I thought all engineers were like this until in my early thirties, when I took out a large bank loan to pay for a top-quality studio and actually experienced what money could buy, if you had it. The attention to detail blew me away, and the guy I worked with, Scott, opened up my eyes to a whole new world of recordings. Rather than just record the band, he would push us to the limit, make suggestions to improve the sound or the performance, spot and correct the smallest intonation issues with the guitars, and take my vocals onto another level. I went into the sessions as a distinctly average singer who was basically winging it, and two weeks later had transformed into an actual proper singer. Scott managed all this through a constant haze of marijuana smoke, and even though we worked twelve-hour sessions, it was always disappointing to have to go home each day.

So when you check out a recording studio, you want to pay at least as much attention to the engineer as the studio itself – probably more. One guy that I met was keenly espousing the many virtues of his cheapish-but-frankly-should-have-been-cheaper studio to me. Now if I'm going to throw thousands of dollars at hiring a studio then I want to hear something that's been made there. Just enough of a song to be able to tell you are at least competent and know how to get a decent vocal sound, to know you can make a quality professional product with me. So I ask the chap if I can hear something, and after much umm-ing and ahh-ing, he inserts a CD in the studio computer and plays me Back in Black by AC/DC. And this album played loud through a nice set of studio monitor speakers sounds fucking brilliant, it has to be said. Admittedly I'm no expert on AC/DC, but it did seem unlikely that they recorded their legendary 50 million selling comeback album with Mutt Lange in this glorified inner city shed. Apart from anything else, when it was recorded in 1980, this dude standing in front of me could have been no more than about twelve years old. And as far as I could tell, he wasn't Mutt Lange. I guess he had nothing he was proud of to play me, which is a bit odd for a recording studio, it seems to me you'd have some sort of showreel at the ready for just these sorts of occasions. I've never forgotten how good the production on Back in Black sounded though, it totally kicked arse.

A year or two after the last recording session in the aforementioned warehouse I had a new band, and this time I was a partner in the running of the band with my co-writer, Robbie. He took lead vocal duties and I was very much content to play guitar and sing harmonies. We spent a day in London looking at a few options for recording, and one studio jumped out because of the engineer. The studio itself was a mess, a ramshackle collection of oddities, old instruments piled up all over the place and it was ominously close to a pub. The engineer however was a likeable old hippy, the studio had a homely smell of sweet cannabis about it, and the last act he'd recorded had been Peter Perrett, former front man of legendary cult band The Only Ones. These last two points very much sold the studio to me. Two things worked against us on this session, the first being that the band was still finding its sound and the second being that the nearest pub was, well, too near. My guitar amps had sounded crap in the studio (remember what I said earlier about being convinced of the merits of cheap gear?) and I ended up using the studio's inhouse Marshall valve amp for the session instead of my crappy Fender transistor amp, and although the result was an improvement, I've never really been a fan of the Marshall sound, and it just felt... wrong. The resulting recording was disappointing, but the upside of this was realising I had to get a new amp. Shortly after, I upgraded to a Fender Twin - next time we were recording, my guitar, for the first time ever, sounded absolutely blisteringly ace.

With my guitar sound sorted and some killer new songs in the repertoire we were ready to record again. Much to our surprise we discovered a cool little studio just up the road from where we were based. Tucked away in the back of a Buckinghamshire village was a quirky piece of land which featured a health club, a recording studio and a large collection of old army tanks. A more incongruous grouping of businesses I have never seen, but it was a neat little studio in a nice country setting which was ideal for a couple of days recording. And the pub was far enough away to make visits unfeasible. The engineer was pretty good and a top chap to boot, and we did three sessions here over the next two years. There was also a resident legendary local musician who lived on the site in a tiny old caravan. He'd sit in on the recording sessions, mostly to keep warm in the comfort of the control room and would spend much of his time apparently sleeping. He'd wake every so often, raise his head, comment on a flaw in the mix with unerring accuracy, before going back to sleep. He also had a knack of waking up at the exact moment that a spliff was sparked up, but as he gifted me a beautiful antique printed Rizla mirror I was more than okay with this – I still have it by the door to my studio today!

These sessions in the late nineties marked my first forays into digital recording. Previously everything I'd done had been recorded to analogue tape, quarter or two inch, neither of which are cheap and would mostly be hired for the duration of the sessions rather than bought and kept. There seemed little point in keeping things at the time, a decision which in the world of massive digital hard drives never really needs to be taken anymore. In this instance we were using DAT (Digital Audio Tape), but still working with an analogue mixing desk rather than a computer-based mixing setup. I was really enjoying the art of mixing by this stage, and in the days before mixing a song on a computer became the norm, creating a mix was an actual performance. Rather than program in all the levels as you go along, automating any changes to the instrument levels, effects, panning etc, we would have to run through the song a number of times, working out what needed to happen beyond the basic instrument track levels. Once you knew what had to be done, you'd attempt a final mix. This would involve perhaps four or five people huddled around the mixing desk, and a sheet of notes confirming what steps needed to be taken in the song. Each person would have a set task or three to do at a given point in the song, e.g. increase volume of acoustic guitar from -3.0 to -1.0 after the intro, mute backing vocals at end of second chorus, slowly pan keyboards from left to right and back again at 2 mins 14 seconds, etc etc. You may have thirty little tweaks to do in one song, and failure to get them all just right would mean starting again. This was sometimes an infuriating process but could be great fun, a real team effort and the sense of achievement when you nailed it was palpable. It's hard not to love the flexibility that an automated computer mix gives you, but I feel something rather special was lost when we stopped mixing in this manner. I was pleasantly surprised while writing this chapter to find that this studio still exists, as I have very fond memories of these sessions, two of which are right up there with the best recordings I've ever done. And I've never come even close to matching the guitar sounds I got there. The tanks have all gone though, which seems a pity.

As the nineties came to a close, computer-based recording setups were becoming viable options, and we smelled a way to save a bit of cash and do our own recordings. What could possibly go wrong? Although the band itself had no money, Robbie had enough to invest in a PC-based recording setup, using an early version of Cubase. He had run his own analogue studio years before, so he was by no means an amateur when it came to recording, but it soon became clear that recording on a computer had very little to do with recording by more traditional means. Or to put it another way, PCs sucked back then, and using them to record was a fucking nightmare of epic proportions. We had a few okay microphones and a small mixing desk to link to the computer, but this is 1999 and Windows at this stage was not the glorious passably-ok-but-a-little-frustrating operating system it is today. Rather it was a bug-ridden piece of crap, about as stable as a one-legged bar stool. We recorded numerous songs, most of which were never seen again as hard drives crashed before we had a chance to click File>Save. It was a gallant attempt at utilising new technology, but in retrospect we should have waited until said technology was a little less crap.

Around this point I relocated to the other side of the world, and I was determined to set myself up with a decent home studio in my new abode. Mindful of recent experience with computers, in 2001 I opted to purchase a Yamaha digital audio workstation instead – basically a self-contained studio built around a traditional mixing desk console, but with a built-in hard drive to record to, and a selection of built-in effects units. It also enabled the user to automate mixes. In short, you could do nearly everything you could do with a computer-based setup, but without the need for a computer. Or so I thought. I mean, it was a stable system that never crashed, was fairly intuitive to use to somebody familiar with to the more hands-on approach of faders and knobs rather than the mouse, and was excellent for recording multiple tracks simultaneously. In fact, it was really very good - almost brilliant. Almost. Where it fell down was that it had no easy way of linking to a computer. All it needed was a simple USB interface enabling you to easily import and export audio tracks in and out of the hard drive, but alas there was not one. I was using a Windows PC for sequenced drum and keyboard loops and the only way to import and export them was a painfully lengthy process involving the built in CD writer. Even this was a minor hassle compared to the joys of PC-based recording. That is until the CD writer broke after a couple of years. At this point I discovered that Yamaha had stopped making the CD writer in question so I couldn't get a replacement, and out the millions of different CD writers out there in the world, there were precisely two that were compatible and they were harder to find than a buried Viking treasure hoard. After many hours on many days fruitlessly searching eBay for parts, I resigned myself to the fact that thousands of dollars of perfectly functional recording equipment had been rendered practically useless by poor decisions from the Yamaha design department. Which bugs me to this day, as you can probably tell. I did manage to record an entire album using the Yamaha, and its portability meant it was great for demoing stuff in the rehearsal room, but it's been gathering dust in my shed for over a decade now.

So I resigned to the inevitable and started working entirely on PC-based recording software. Surely things were much better now than a few years previously when recording on computers went so horribly wrong for me? Nope. I will attempt to gloss over the horror of the next couple of years as I really don't want to relive the frustration any more than necessary. I estimate that during the period of 2001-2008, especially the latter years when I was forced into recording on a PC rather than just using one for editing and programming, I probably spent upwards of ninety percent of the time trying to get computers to work properly and stop crashing, and less than ten percent actually using them for their designated purpose. This happened across several PCs, regardless of which software I was using – Logic, Cubase, Fruity Loops, ProTools – and regardless of whether the operating system was Windows 98, Windows 2000 or Windows XP. These were computers dedicated to recording too, and setup as such, it wasn't as if they were being used as a multi-purpose PC for numerous other applications. It was partly as a result of this experience that I ended up breaking the bank and using a top-class studio facility for the next album I recorded.

But recording in a top-class establishment with a top-class engineer can be a mixed blessing. Don't get me wrong, we spent ten days recording an album that is probably the best thing I've done, sonically speaking. And as I mentioned before, I felt like I came out of the sessions as a proper singer thanks to Scott, the engineer, as well as learning a huge amount about how to record properly. It was a brilliant experience. But man, when you're working with people who are used to making hit records, you better up your game accordingly. I think my drummer at the time, John, is probably still traumatised to this day by the pressure he was put under to play perfectly in time – which to be fair, shouldn't be a big ask for a drummer, especially one in his late forties. The first day was a complete write-off as the tempos were all over the place, so we started again and forced John to play to a click track (which is essentially a metronome) to keep in perfect time. He got there in the end, but I think it took four twelve-hour days in the end to record ten drum tracks, which was, um, expensive. When I got around to doing my guitars, Scott was unhappy with the intonation on both my acoustic and electric guitars. You don't tend to notice this in a live environment, but under the microscope in this situation they didn't cut the mustard, so I ended up having to hire an acoustic guitar from a local guitar shop[55], and use one of the studio's own electric guitars. Basically nothing was getting past Scott unless it was absolutely spot on, which I think is what any engineer worth his salt should be like. He forced us to make as good a record as we possibly could, and as we went forward the knock-on effect both live and on future recording projects was immense. Although John never completely nailed the knack of playing to the click track. In the end we settled on a routine of recording me playing the song on an acoustic guitar in time to the click track, and then he'd record his drums to fit my guitar – without the click track! A reasonably effective approach, but enormously time-consuming, and something is definitely missing doing it this way as compared to playing live with the band. But if you're doing anything other than a purely live recording, a solid predictable tempo on the drums is an absolute

---

55 And boy was it good. A beautiful 1975 Martin D28. I've never heard a guitar quite like it, it positively sang. Much to my delight, seven years later the shop finally agreed to sell it to me!

must. This recording session also marked the first time I'd recorded a violin, and here enters the second musician to be rather traumatised by the whole experience. We had a chap called Martin who'd come down to a rehearsal one day to tentatively test whether a violin player might work as a full-time addition to the line-up, and I got him to drop in for a couple of hours to add some parts to three songs. I'd struggled to hear him clearly at the rehearsal amongst the volume of the rest of the band, but I'd thought the bits I did hear were very promising, and he talked the talk. And if I wanted to sound like The Waterboys then I need a fiddle right?[56] I should have been a bit more diligent, but I thought it couldn't do any harm. Scott and I sat in the control room getting ready as Martin warmed up, clearly nervous, not a good thing in someone whom on closer inspection now that I've got to know him a little seems to have some not insignificant anxiety issues actually. Anyway, it turns out that despite Martin being in his fifties and talking the talk, he's never been in a recording studio before, so he's nervous with a dose of extra nervous thrown in for good measure. Coupled with that was the fact that violin is an incredibly unforgiving instrument – stunningly beautiful like no other when played with consummate skill and soul[57], yet ear-achingly horrific when played with anything less[58]. And as we've already learned, Scott is an absolute perfectionist. Martin's takes started off badly, got worse and worse despite all attempts to cajole a performance out of him for over an hour, and ended with Martin insisting that we

---

56 <Narrator's voice>: he needed a lot more than a fiddle.

57 See Martin Hayes, or Steve Wickham.

58 Like a surprising number of violinists actually. Perhaps the price God extracts for the musician getting the privilege to play a) an instrument with such sublime possibility and b) one that is light as a feather, in a handy small case and able to be plugged into the desk directly at the gig thus getting you out of the tiresome task of carrying an amp around, not to mention buying one... is that if you don't put full effort into this instrument, you will sound not just bad, but offensively so, possibly blood-curdlingly so.

didn't know what we were doing and it wasn't out of tune, it's the mixolydian scale you idiots and us politely trying to say that no, the scale is fine you're just not hitting the notes, it's your fingers, your intonation, and him listening back to tracks and telling us they were fine really pretty good actually and us beginning to laugh thinking he was joking and an awkward moment as we realise he's not joking and he realises we think he's shit. But it's very difficult to be entirely honest in these situations without feeling terrible about it, especially as you seem to be unintentionally pushing someone's anxiety levels into uncomfortable new areas and the air is beginning to feel a bit... mental breakdowny. I pulled myself together and said okay, we'll work with what we've got, and he went home, both parties feeling much worse about themselves than they had two hours ago. To this day I shudder if anyone ever mentions the mixolydian scale. Scott and I smoked a joint and had a bit of a laugh as we reviewed a slightly odd and comical recording session, and he told me that experiment had cost me nearly $400 while trying to keep a straight face. I never saw Martin again, but over the ensuing months I heard from a couple of mutual acquaintances that the experience of working with us that day had been absolute torture for him, and he had vowed never to go into a studio again! Sorry about that Martin.

Revelling in the freedom to spend money that was loaned money and therefore not real money, John and I went to mix the album in England, staying and working with my old friend George[59] for a couple of weeks. George had been getting a lot of experience mixing over the years, and I'd really liked the sound of some of the mixes that he'd done recently for his own band, so I was keen to work with someone

---

59 He of the farm-based rehearsal room, remember?

who I knew could do a good job and was also one of my closest friends. As it transpired, George did ten days mixing for practically nothing, so even factoring in the cost of flights it still worked out cheaper than mixing it with Scott at the studio where we'd done the recording. George's studio was situated in the beautiful Oxfordshire countryside and we stayed there during a lovely summer, producing some great mixes and catching up with some old friends – which just about offset John and I having to live in each other's pockets for four long-haul flights, ten nights sharing the studio bedroom, eight hours plus of mixing every day, along with most evenings!

Doing this album gave me a nice break from the rage-inducing computer recording experience at home, and I decided to splash out on an Apple iMac. I'd never used a Mac before, but mixing the last album with George on his Mac with Logic software had been a joy, so I convinced myself, rightly for once, that this plan would work. Who could ever have guessed that you get what you pay for?[60] I eagerly unboxed my shiny new Apple, which just exuded quality from the packaging inwards. I turned it on, installed the Logic Pro studio software and connected my old Tascam external soundcard. Even including the hour or so waiting on software installation and the forty minutes I spent failing to work out how to install the soundcard before realising that the Mac had already done it for me the moment I plugged it in, I had a fully functional recording set up within two hours, and it worked perfectly without so much as a single crash for a good five years or more. Seeing how smoothly this all worked was hard to believe at first and Apple moved into an elite minority of large corporations that I felt only goodwill towards, and cemented the

---

60 Not me, obviously.

place of Bill Gates, owner and face of Microsoft, in the top echelon of people whom I'd like to kick in the balls in reward for all the pain they've caused me over the years. Somewhere inside is a small voice telling me that Bill is probably not directly to blame, but I'm pretty sure I could ignore that voice if the opportunity ever arises. In time however I realised that while Apple's products were very good at this sort of thing, everything tended to go awry when the time came for something to be upgraded. In my case, I unwittingly installed an upgrade to the Apple operating system which, rather than being the simple upgrade I was expecting, turned out to be an entirely new operating system. I forget which one it was – I think I had OSX Snow Leopard, and had purposefully ignored upgrades to OSX Sea Lion and OSX Tasmanian Devil, but they managed to sneak OSX Mallard Duck past me. Oh well I thought, a new operating system might be nice, what's the worst that could happen? Well there are always worse scenarios that could happen, but what did happen feels like it's still up to its neck in it in the shit-heap of worsts' that can happen. The new system was incompatible with my version of the Logic software and... look, I'm not going to bore you with the details, I'll just say if you get a computer-based studio facility working, then don't mess with it – if it ain't broke, don't fix it. I had a friend whose studio was running on Windows 98 with an equally old version of Cubase, but it worked just fine for over 15 years because he never updated anything! That is *exactly* what you want.

Having a decent setup at home became an indispensable tool in the end. I'd pay to use a studio with a live room just for drums or a basic live band setup, but then edit all those tracks and record things like vocals and acoustic instruments at home, saving a small fortune.

This started getting tricky when I had children. As a parent, you spend a fair amount of the first couple of years tiptoeing around the house trying to make as little noise as possible, lest you wake the little angel that you've just spent an hour and a half rocking on your arm and feeding in an attempt to get them to sleep. So recording becomes nigh on impossible. I got into the habit of taking the bare essentials of my recording gear to the houses of other band members who had yet to suffer the blessings of parenthood, setting up temporary recording studios and getting a well-deserved break[61] from the kids into the bargain. I got well-practiced in a quick studio setup and strip down and did a lot of recording this way, but of late I look at the amount of tangled cables, drives and devices that seem so settled where they are in my house and think sod it, I'll bribe the missus to take the kids out for the day and I'll record people here.

One thing I've never really enjoyed doing is recording vocals at home. I can get a very good sound, but that's really not the issue. In the live room or vocal booth of your commercial recording studio, you can sing your heart out at the top of your lungs all day long, safe in the knowledge that it's just you, an engineer and a sound proof room, and I bloody love doing that - revelling in the freedom to make as much noise and as many ill-conceived experimentations and awful screw-ups as you like, knowing that nobody can hear you other than the engineer. In my home studio however, the window is only a metre or so away from the driveway of the house next door, a driveway where the family and their friends like to congregate for regular cigarettes. It's much harder to concentrate on your singing when you're keeping an ear out for neighbours, and while your singing may sound great

---

61 I've not checked, but I'm sure this is exactly what my wife would think.

in the context of the backing track in your headphones, all that the neighbour hears is the voice with absolutely no context, often repeating a line or two over and over until you get it just right, and frankly you feel like a bit of a dick in this scenario. And you can't do it if anyone else is home – the vocal mics are so sensitive that you need almost complete silence, which is not what children are designed for, or wives for that matter. Even when I do get a couple of hours with everybody else out of the house, the proximity of freeway, train line and flight path make my home studio an enormously frustrating place to work!

The last time I recorded an album with a full band was a mish mash of all these previous options really. We did about four days recording the main band parts at a lovely recording studio with a chap called Jason, a very talented engineer with a great track record, and a lovely guy too. Then I took all the parts home and over the next couple of months added all the backing vocals and a few additional instruments, as well as editing all the raw parts we'd recorded with Jason. This was the last time I recorded with John on drums. While he was doing much better with his timing by this stage, it was still a little off-track at times and I spent far too many evenings painstakingly making adjustments to hi-hats and kick drums until everything sat just right. After this I swore never again, and replaced him shortly after, a painful thing to do to a friend but an incredible relief in the end (for him too I suspect). Anyway, editing all the parts down to the bits I needed took a long time, but it pays dividends to do it at home – by the time I went back into Jason's studio it was a case of simply loading up all the parts and starting to mix, saving many days and many dollars in the process. The whole album was mixed in four days and sounded great. I had a fantastic time mixing it, and Jason's expertise was surprisingly affordable. With the cheaper studios you might pay four to five hundred dollars for an eight-hour day, and Jason charged seven hundred and fifty – but his working days were at least twelve hours long, and on a couple of days we ended up going for sixteen hours straight. I'd learnt very quickly that I could trust his judgement implicitly on everything except perhaps the backing vocals, so I was able to squeeze in a fair few naps on the very comfortable studio sofas. I repeated this technique on a more stripped back album a couple of years later, but this time did all the actual recording with my own facilities and just mixed it with Jason. Again, the results were excellent, and I'd managed to reduce the costs of making a quality album down to about four thousand dollars all up, not a bad effort.

Ultimately, although I thoroughly enjoy it, I've never quite managed to master the recording studio. I've learnt an awful lot from people far more gifted than me and I can put together a decent enough recording, a decent mix and do a passable mastering of the track as well, but I've never quite had the inclination or tools to really nail the process. It takes a hell of a lot of time to really master the skills and equipment of the engineer, and every day spent on the more mundane stuff, like messing around with an assortment of different compressors trying to perfect the kick drum sound, is a day you could be spending doing frankly far more interesting things, like mowing the lawn or plucking your eyebrows. I've never quite managed to commit to the mundane, so in the end my own production capabilities have remained firmly in the experienced well-meaning amateur category. I've recorded three albums that have been mixed by experienced award-winning professionals, and it's safe to say that sonically they sit comfortably at the top of my recorded output. If you want something done properly, don't do it yourself.

10.
PROMOTING THE BAND

THE POSTER AND THE FLYER

The poster and the flyer have traditionally been the number one promotional tools for any band, an allegedly valuable pair of marketing techniques that the general public have been ignoring and throwing on the floor for centuries. I suspect that their main use is actually as a general branding exercise rather than an effective seller of tickets for your show, nevertheless you can't do a show without a poster. While I've been around long enough to remember making hand-drawn posters and flyers without the aid of computer technology, I'm also thankfully young enough to have had access to a photocopier from the start of my career. I seem to recall getting my Dad to photocopy my first flyers when he was at work – it was many years before I found myself in a workplace kitted out with a full set of print and copy equipment, ready to utilise in the name of band marketing when the boss was out at lunch. Handmade posters were fun to make to be honest – most bands tend to have someone with some degree of artistic talent inhouse, so the issue with production is usually motivational rather than skills. I think my first efforts were actually a combination of handwritten text coupled with fancy borders courtesy of Letraset. Letraset, for those of you who have never had the pleasure, were a company that made sheets of typefaces and images that you could rub onto paper, giving you the same effect as if you had your own desktop publishing software and printing setup[62]. As computer technology developed, unless you were at the forefront of graphic design, you might find yourself lucky enough to have access to a basic word processing package with <gasp> three of four different fonts. This was, however, not necessarily a step forward from the handmade production – apart from anything else, print resolution tended to be shocking and not much use for doing anything other than printing a barely readable invoice, on top of which the printer was more than likely a dot matrix anyway. The good old dot matrix was brilliant if you actually did want to print a barely readable invoice, but not exactly poster-worthy, although the paper would usually have those perforated edges which were fairly satisfying to tear off, so there is that. Man, I remember the joy of getting my first access to a laser printer circa 1997, and discovering that you could actually print vaguely professional and usable documents. At last!

Handmade posters were pretty well consigned to history by the time that Windows PCs began to gain popularity. Instead of pissing around for hours with Letraset or pens and rulers you could waste your time pissing around with early versions of Paint or Word instead, which were far more frustrating. I mean it was pretty exciting to realise that you could use all the potential capability of Word to help with posters – an assortment of fonts, decent typesetting, the ability to add images and, most awesome of all, the wonders of clipart, but the reality was that Word was a complete piece of shit and pretty much anything you wanted to do was a bit of a nightmare. As Douglas

---

[62] Presuming that your set up featured a printer that regularly missed off parts of random letters, and software with very dubious kerning capabilities.

Adams once said, "we are stuck with technology when what we really want is just stuff that works". Early clipart really was appalling, but for a while the novelty value overrode the naffness of it. Although in time it did improve, and clipart went from laughably bad to its-a-bit-rubbish-but-it'll-do. It's important to realise too that nobody I knew actually had their own computer to spend time doing all this stuff on – it all had to be done in moments of snatched time at work by any band members who actually had a job (far from a given), and more specifically an office job with their own computer. And then you also needed access to a decent printer, so you could print a master copy in A4 to take to the photocopy shop and get some A3 versions done. Anything larger than that was prohibitively expensive.

By the early twenty first century I had finally got my hands my own computer, and more importantly a copy of Photoshop, at which point I was actually able to do some decent designs without swearing profusely at the software. Well, less swearing anyway. Printing was still an issue though. A lack of anybody yet inventing USB sticks or decent internet capability meant that getting your design to a printing shop invariably meant burning the damn thing to CD and then watching in horror as the printer added twenty bucks to your bill to cover the twenty seconds it took them to transfer the data from your CD to their computer, and then produce copies with colours bearing only the slightest of passing resemblance to your original design. Then a stroke of luck – a band member working in a large company with numerous A3 colour laser printers! Wow. We made the most of this for many years and saved a fortune in printing costs, meaning a large Australian telecommunications company effectively unwittingly sponsored us for a while, whilst receiving nothing back in return for their kindness.

And that's the thing with posters. Unless you're lucky, like in the instance above, they cost a fair bit of money to produce. We've already established that most gigs at pub and club level pay very little, yet many venues will insist on a bunch of colour A3 posters being provided by the band. A3 is a suitable size to put up in a venue, but no use whatsoever if you want to poster the neighbourhood. Your average poster that has been stuck up on a convenient wall advertising the latest Pink tour is A0 size, which is eight times bigger than A3, and correspondingly pricier. If you actually want to do a decent, noticeable poster campaign for a gig, it better be a decent paying gig. And therein lies the heart of the problem for any band - you can't afford the promotional outlay necessary to pull the crowds big enough to enable you to afford the promotional outlay necessary to pull the crowds.

Flyers are far cheaper to produce than posters, as they're that much smaller. You'll get two or more likely four flyers to one page of A4, and A4 printing is cheap enough to manage, especially as anyone with a job in an office - or a friend with a job in an office - can do them. The fun bit is sitting down and cutting them all out! But flyers don't hand themselves out, and the pleasure of handing out flyers to punters leaving a venue late at night or perhaps dropping them off at various music shops or cafes is a dubious one at best. Many years ago I would happily travel around the city and drop off posters and flyers to an assortment of independent record shops, cafes and clothing stores, but eventually capitalism took over and screwed everything, as is its wont. I found most of these stores now refusing my posters, as they now only put up posters distributed by certain companies, i.e. those that paid a fee for the real estate of the shop's wall to promote their stable of decidedly un-independent bands. Sigh.

The realisation that posters were a branding exercise rather than a targeted marketing campaign led me to think that I could actually make some posters for fake gigs, which progressed to fake gigs at fake venues. Nobody ever complained to the band about us not turning up for a gig, and nobody ever contacted us to ask where the hell the venue on the poster actually was, which sort of proved a point[63]. We then stuck a bunch of posters up with no dates on them at all, not even a band name – just a logo. Sometimes we'd go busking, and people would see the logo on a CD in the guitar case and click – "hey, you're those guys, from the posters, I see them everywhere, I wondered what they were all about!". It didn't make them buy a CD, but it was probably the biggest impact that our posters had ever made. Sadly.

Spider and I once hit upon the idea of avoiding the cost of printing altogether and making some truly enormous posters with spray paint, stencils and large roles of plain paper. I think the biggest one we made was about two metres high and a mighty twelve metres wide. The homemade aesthetic became a design feature rather than looking like a cheap cop-out, and they looked fucking great once affixed to a suitable wall – to which they would stay affixed in some cases for many years, due to a particularly great paste recipe that we stumbled upon.

---

63 Although the jury is out on whether the point proved was that posters were a branding exercise only, or that we simply had no fans. Perhaps a little of both?

Not that this was easy of course. As I mentioned earlier, Spider was only too happy to drive around the city with me after midnight, with a bunch of posters and a bucket of homemade wallpaper paste, and the two of us went on many a mission to affix our artwork to the most visible and unlikely spots possible. Essential requirements for such a mission include a bucket of paste, a couple of huge paintbrushes (or brooms for the really large posters), a stepladder and some rags[64]. Spending money on actual wallpaper paste was pointless, as great results could be achieved with cornflour[65]. I could offer many pieces of advice on technique for this sort of mission, but the main one would be to just make damn sure you don't spill that bucket of paste on the floor of the car if you have any intention of ever selling the car, or indeed using it again. These late-night trips were always fun. The adrenalin is always running high as you're keeping an eye out for The Pigs - it's pretty hard to do a runner with a bucket of paste, a roll of posters and a stepladder. And finding innovative spots is a real challenge. You want somewhere noticeable, but unlikely to get you prosecuted for vandalism[66]. You also want to avoid the normal poster spots so that the commercial poster crews which go around the city every night don't simply poster straight over yours. For a long time we made a point of scarpering when these crews were spotted, as we'd heard tales of their mafia-like approach to the poster industry and we didn't want to be pissing them off. Then they caught us in the act one night as we made a piss-poor attempt to get one of our six-metre-long posters affixed high up on a wall above the paying customer's posters. Nervously readying our excuses as they approached, we were somewhat gobsmacked when they congratulated us on our work and

---

64 Do NOT forget the rags

65 That is as long as you don't make the mistake I once did and buy gluten-free cornflour.

66 It's tricky to deny responsibility for something that has your band name all over it, and which also gives an exact date and location of where you can be found.

assisted us in our postering with their superior knowledge, skills and equipment. Which was... unexpected!

Believe it or not, there are people that simply refuse to honour the Posterer's Code. It's a simple code that is incredibly easy to follow – don't remove posters, or put your posters up over posters, for shows that have yet to take place. Nevertheless there are people out there that take pleasure in either maliciously destroying your hard work or simply postering straight over it. The people that do this fall into two categories. First are the bands that think they're more important than you, and these bands really should know better. Secondly are the self-appointed neighbourhood guardians who, whilst completely fine with the likes of Harry Styles or Beyoncé having their posters on every free bit of wall going, are simply not going to stand for a bunch of local reprobates having the nerve to try and promote themselves, and they will do their best to tear down these outrageous affronts to their bizarrely misaligned sense of community spirit. I can't imagine what sort of knob feels the need to do this, but they are out there, I've encountered them many times. Beware.

THE PHOTOSHOOT

Photoshoots are fun. Sort of. Dressing up in your finest, going out to a good location and then posing like a bit of twat is not exactly hard work, although like anything else that you're not getting paid for it's a bugger to get everybody together at the same time, and obviously this gets exponentially worse depending on how many people are in your band. Likewise, the more people in the band, the harder it is to get a decent shot with everyone looking acceptably acceptable. And as you've decided to get a boyfriend/girlfriend/mate to take the photos instead of an actual professional photographer[67], the chances of getting a really good shot are reduced further by virtue of the fact that they don't know what they're doing and their equipment is substandard. Even if they have decent equipment they probably don't know how to work it properly. This is mitigated a little with digital technology, as you can now easily manipulate a pretty average photo into something just about usable. It's only when you compare your work to the stuff done by the real professionals that you realise the quantum leap in quality betwixt the two.

Personally I'd always try and find a rather private secluded setting. I've done a couple of shoots in some very public spots, and there are few things as likely to adversely affect the shot than a bunch of curious strangers watching on and shouting abuse and/or "hilarious" "witticisms". A common theme for the band photoshoot, and generally suitably secluded, is the backdrop of industrial decay. I don't really know why. Perhaps it's the large number of such sites, easily found in any town or city. Perhaps it's because these places are the antithesis of glamour, an appealing notion for bands that wish to distance themselves from anything glamorous, or for bands that wish to offset their own shiny colourfulness against something that is quite the opposite. Either way, it's a popular trope. One of my bands was based in a town with a long-abandoned soft drinks factory. The place was huge, fairly accessible and looked great. I can't speak for the female of the species, but I can say that pretty much every young male's spirit of adventure is awoken with the possibility of exploring

---

[67] This is absolutely what has happened, there is no way you've paid for an actual professional.

these sort of places – who knows what cool stuff you'll find, what cool stuff you'll get to destroy? Dead bodies, suitcases full of unmarked bills, large stashes of long-abandoned drugs... the possibilities are exciting, albeit distant. But at the very least you can get some decent photos. So off we went, three young men dressed for a photoshoot[68] along with my girlfriend and her camera. There was a large metal gate to climb over, topped off with barbed wire, but once that obstacle was traversed we were in. The site must have been at least ten acres in size, so there was plenty of ground to cover. We wandered around looking for the best spot for some photos, but in the end we just kept taking photos all the way around, as pretty much every spot was a good one. Many other people had been here in the preceding years, and I don't think there was a single wall left untouched by graffiti, a single windowpane left unbroken or indeed anything that hadn't been either partly or completely trashed. Perfect really. After a while we noticed that a handful of kids had been watching us. We ignored them initially, but they grew keener for attention as the afternoon wore on, and we politely told them to fuck off. When this didn't work, we tried telling them to fuck off in a slightly less polite manner. Now, these kids were all of about ten years old. And we were all in our early twenties. And we knew, from being ten years old at some point ourselves in the not too distant past, that when a bunch of grown men tell you to fuck off, fuck off is exactly what you do. And indeed they did. Or so we thought. We got on with some more photos. However, what the kids had actually done was go and get a bunch more mates. As we stood outside taking the last of the pictures, the kids reappeared around the corner. Except that instead of it being three or four ten-year olds, it was now about twenty kids, many in their teens, and all of them carrying bricks, metal poles or lumps of

---

68 Which is categorically not the same as being dressed for exploring an industrial wasteland.

timber. Which put us in a bit of a quandary. On the one hand this is a bunch of kids and we're a bunch of adults. On the other, they're all armed and marching towards you. Even if you stand your ground, you're going to get physically hurt, and on balance this was a worse option than getting your pride hurt. I mean pride is all well and good, but it doesn't bleed. And in small town England, kids like this are generally little bastards that won't hesitate to cause serious injury and that will bloody well love the opportunity to tell their mates that they beat up a bunch of adults, especially a bunch of poseurs like us. Deciding very quickly that we had more than enough photos now thank you very much, we headed back to the gate. Slowly at first, but as they smelt the fear they got more confident and started yelling that we were going to be killed. And as we neared the gate, they realised that we were in danger of getting away, so they charged. There was no wait-until-you-see-the-whites-of-their-eyes-lads-stand-your-ground moment from us. Cowardice was overwhelmingly the sensible option, so we legged it to the gate, tore our clothes to pieces as we clambered over the barbed wire, leapt into the car and raced off. The gate was our saviour in the end, as half these kids were too small to get over it any time soon, and it was very much an all-or-nothing style attack. We escaped with our lives, which was all that mattered, but our egos were decidedly battered, and we agreed to never speak of the incident again. Oops, sorry chaps. Got some good photos though.

There is a direct correlation between photo shoots and band members leaving. The more effort you put into a photo shoot in terms of location, props, imagery etc, the more likely someone is to leave the band in the coming weeks. This has been proven several times to me, and it took me a while to realise that this makes pretty much no difference. Sure, it's an incredible annoyance, but unless you're Led Zeppelin or The Beatles nobody will notice that the dude second on the right is Joe Bloggs and not John Smith, so it doesn't actually matter one bit. But YOU know. And it WILL bug you. This is of course all the more likely to happen if you've arranged a professional photographer[69].

I feel a little sorry for professional photographers. I've known a few, and never bothered to ask them to do a photo shoot for me. This is not because I'm a really lovely bloke, sensitive to the needs of the people I know, who would never try and scrounge a freebie from a mate. I absolutely would try and scrounge a freebie from a mate[70]. But in the case of photographers, they have all pre-empted me by complaining about the number of people that try and get a free photo shoot, especially bands and weddings. Oh really mate, that's terrible, yeah I'd never ask that of you[71].

The first time we did a shoot with digital technology was not a productive occasion. We had a manager who had just got himself a digital camera and was accordingly extremely pleased with himself. We're back in the mid-nineties here, with dial-up internet and floppy disks, so none of the modern-day advantages of file transferring and manipulation were really available. But, and this is once again the key point, a digital camera did mean no film and no costly film development, so digital was clearly a very appealing option. We

---

69 Which of course you haven't, so there's that at least.
70 Just ask any of the mechanics I've known.
71 Bugger.

arranged a location, and in an unprecedented act of preparation and professionalism, not to mention expense[72], lighting and dry ice was hired. Hell, I even bought a new shirt[73]. We had some fun, got some cool shots and looked forward to seeing and using the end results. We never used the end results. The camera was cleverly set to a low resolution, so while the shots looked good on the camera viewfinder, they were entirely unprintable. In fact, the resolution was so low, that they were completely useless if you wanted to view them at any size larger than the camera's 2x1½ inch viewfinder, and we decided that on balance it was impractical to take the camera along in person to show the pictures to anybody who wanted to see them.

After a while I pretty much abandoned the idea of proper photoshoots entirely. As smartphones and their cameras got better, I'd just get someone to take a snap of the band before a gig, or somewhere on the road. This was a very liberating decision, and even if the photos were a bit crap they were at least real, and people like stuff that's real. And to be honest, I think a decent live shot is a far better bet. Although getting a decent live shot is surprisingly hard, especially one of the entire band, and be assured that if you use a photo of, say, just the singer and guitarist, the rest of the band will be pissed off. The drummer will inevitably be obscured by cymbals if he makes it into the shot at all, which is fairly upsetting for the drummer but, well, nobody really cares about that other than the drummer, and the drummer's partner. But for a good live shot you do need a good photographer, or at least a good camera. For a couple of years a partner of one band member liked to dabble in photography,

---

[72] On the managers behalf. I mean come on, you don't think we paid for that do you?

[73] From a charity shop.

and he at least met the second of the aforementioned criteria. What he perhaps lacked in experience and natural talent he certainly made up for in enthusiasm, and his prolific output meant I'd regularly get handed a DVD with five hundred or more photos on it from the gig, or if he'd come along to a festival it'd be literally thousands of photos. I don't want to appear ungrateful, this really was pretty awesome, but man, it took hours and hours to sort through all these photos, picking out the one in every hundred that was actually useable, and ignoring the fifty percent that were photos of his missus smiling at him from the stage! For a while we were also cursed by the White Plastic Chair. For some reason there would always be one of these chairs at festivals – or maybe it was always the same one, I don't know. It's technically possible I suppose. Anyway, the chair would somehow always find its way on stage without anybody noticing. I don't know why. I don't know how. After a while the band implemented a pre-gig policy of doing a quick White Plastic Chair scan of the stage before we went on, to confirm the absence of said chair. And even after I'd give the stage the all-clear, somehow the fucking thing would be there in the photos, staring back at me and laughing as it ruined an otherwise great picture. This happened so often that I began to think these chairs were actually sentient, and capable of moving under their own volition. And on a stage that is predominantly dark, with a black backdrop, the White Plastic Chair stands out like the proverbial dog's bollocks.

Talking of live shots, I've done loads of gigs, especially at festivals, where you'd see from the stage a photographer doing their work, snapping away, usually with a few lanyards around their neck identifying themselves as someone working, rather than being a very keen and prepared fan. I've often wondered what happens to all these photos. There must be thousands of photos of my bands out there, somewhere, unpublished, unused, unlabelled. Only on very rare occasions have I seen them pop up on a festival's social media page or website. Although there was one set of photos of us that were absolutely great, that I came across on a festival's Facebook feed. I downloaded them and posted them on Twitter, and a day or two later received a furious message from the photographer demanding that we take them down immediately or we'd be hearing from his lawyer. Didn't we know we could buy the originals at only $50 each, he said, as if $50 was small change to a band rather than half of our profits from the last quarter? Perhaps it's best that I don't ever see the photos after all.

THE VIDEO SHOOT

All of the videos I've ever done have been crap. But also really good fun, for the most part. Filming a video clip falls somewhere between a photo shoot and a recording studio session – it's quite good fun dressing up and posing/pissing about a bit, but there are long periods of boredom too, and the drummer will do your head in.

Much like recording, creating videos is something that you can do yourself, technically speaking, and save a bit of cash. And much like recording, although you can do it yourself - technically speaking - it's best to involve someone who actually knows what they are doing and perhaps spend a bit of cash. And again, like recording where you can take the attitude of nah that take will do, we can always fix it up in the mix, with video you can take the attitude of nah, that take will do, we can always fix it up in post-production. But just like recording, this choice will always be regretted.

Now that I think about it, I've never done a full video clip with a professional team from start to finish. I've done three or four video clips, as well as a couple of live shoots, where I've hired the pros to do the camera work for me, which is nice – working with people who actually consider things like lighting, make-up, decent hardware, and aren't just winging it. But in all but one case the editing and post-production have been done inhouse. I had a keyboard player named Tom that dabbled in video a little, and he took charge of the projects, managing them and taking care of everything bar the actual filming. He didn't do a bad job in fairness, but on both occasions he clearly bit off far more than he could chew, resulting in massive delays in getting the final product. The first time, we got the video about three months after the single was released, which was about six months after we filmed it. This was a three-minute video clip, and the mathematicians amongst you will quickly spot that this worked out at a production rate of one day for every second of footage, which is the sort of work-rate that only a builder would be proud of. I should have learned my lesson here, but when the next video clip came up a year or two later, it was instead Tom insisting that he had learned his lessons, and this one would come together much quicker. Of course, now that he was more experienced, Tom felt confident in adding some CGI elements to the clip. This time the video was again shot three months before the release of the single, but this time it wasn't completed for a mammoth fourteen months, nearly an entire year after the single was released, rendering it pretty much bloody useless from a promotional perspective. And even the slackest builder would have been ashamed[74] with that rate of progress (2.36 days per second of footage!).

So when the offer came along from a senior film student to not only film a clip for us, but to do everything else into the bargain, I jumped at the chance. We spent a fun day filming in the countryside, trespassing on some private land so that we could use a beautiful and little-known run-down old building from the days of the nineteenth century settlers in Australia. When the location was scouted it was clearly perfect for what we had in mind, although as an amateur scouting for locations with just my dog, I found it was fairly easy to overlook the sort of logistical problems that, while not an issue for myself and my dog, can prove problematic when accompanied by seven other people, assorted guitar cases and drums, a smoke machine, bags full of clothes, camera flight cases, tripods, lighting and a diesel-powered generator. Like for example climbing over the edge of a bridge and clambering down a steep thirty-foot slope, crossing a river via stepping-stones before hacking your way through half a mile of dense bushland. Also a handy tip – if you're trespassing on someone else's land, don't bring a diesel-powered generator or a smoke machine, at least not if you have any designs on keeping your presence undetected. While the whole project cost only about a hundred dollars, we were let down rather by the senior film student getting a much more junior film student to do the final edit, which was a bit rubbish. Once more my steadfast refusal to recognise the unquestionable authority of the law of Thou Gets What Thou Pays For came back to haunt me. Then again it was only about a month

---

74 Yeah like fuck would they.

late in completion, so I was slowly but surely edging closer to the goal of getting a video completed in time for a song's release.

Now that I think about, this wasn't the first video that involved an element of trespassing[75]. On the first video that Tom had produced for us (eventually) we'd been looking for a large room with plain white walls to film in. A friend of Tom's had said he could get us into a room at his university that fitted the bill, a room that they indeed often used for filming. By "getting us in" I presumed he meant "arrange with the necessary authorities to borrow on the weekend", but what he actually meant was "break in via a side door on the weekend and hope nobody spots us". This approach actually worked up to a point – nobody did spot us, and we got some good footage. Unfortunately I put a slight spanner in the works when I walked backwards while filming a vocal shot, misjudged my whereabouts, and stuck my foot right through the wall, leaving a sizeable hole and some not unconvincing evidence that perhaps someone had maybe been using the room that day. Despite my protestations that having broken into the room without being caught we couldn't possibly be held responsible for the damage, Tom and his friend successfully guilt-tripped me into promising to repair the damage I had caused. Which meant on Sunday morning I had to pop down the hardware store, purchase some filler and some paint, gather up a not inconsiderable amount of newspaper to plug a hole the size of a size 11 shoe, and break in once again to the university to repair the damage of the initial breaking and entering. Of course plaster tends to take a while to dry, so not only did I have to break in and fill and plaster the hole, I then had to come back later and break in for a third time so that I

---

[75] Actually the words "an", "element" and "of" are entirely redundant here

could sand down the plaster when it had dried, and then paint it. I have to say, the security at the university was clearly in need of an overhaul.

I was beginning to amass a fair amount of video footage, predominantly live footage, and eventually decided that I'd try my hand at video editing myself. I actually found it much simpler than mixing music for the most part, although I was ill-prepared for just how much computer processing power I would need[76]. I was also unprepared for the amount of digital file formats for video. With music you're usually working with a .wav file or a .aiff file for high quality sounds, perhaps converting to .mp3 for the purpose of emailing or using on portable devices. There are other options, but those three will steer you home just fine. Video however has more file formats available than there are stars in the known universe. And there are more stars in the universe than there are grains of sand on all the beaches of our humble home planet[77]. For every actual file format there are a myriad of different codecs[78] available, and each one has its own range of possible settings. It's utterly baffling, and to the untrained producer the only thing you can rely on is that you'll choose the wrong one. And when you eventually do stumble upon the right one, it won't be the right one for every given situation. And the best results can give you file sizes that you could upload to YouTube but only if you don't want to use your internet connection

---

[76] Producing some half decent results with some home movie footage for a few minutes of finished film seems to require approximately the same amount of processing power that Google use for their entire search operation.

[77] Or so they say. I've looked into the theory behind this and to be honest it's not overly convincing, as we're working with estimates so broad that the terms "complete guesswork" and "you haven't really got a clue have you" do come to mind. Either way however, there are still more video formats.

[78] For those of you who don't know what a codec is, I'm afraid I can't help you.

for anything else over the next four months. But for all that, when I did finally decide to just do all the video creation and editing myself, I did at least manage to complete them in time to release on the same date as the song.

I should generally ignore many of the ideas that I think up, and a great example of this is the idea I had to film a multi-camera shot of a gig and edit it myself. Oh dear God. At great expense I hired a crew to shoot an entire show with four cameras, and another person to record multi-track audio. I figured we could probably come up with a decent live CD/DVD package, but my ambitions were, er, ambitious. And blimey, editing four different cameras worth of footage from a ninety-minute performance, all synched up to the same audio track, is a logistical and processing-power nightmare of enormous proportions, that I would never ever attempt again, ever[79]. This is the sort of project where you quickly realise the benefits that a proper lighting rig and operator would bring to the party, not to mention a crowd of several thousand rather than two hundred, and a stage raised more than a foot from the floor. And when you finally do finish putting the video together, all that's left is the small matter of sorting out the audio track, which essentially means mixing a ninety-minute album. Urgh. They say most of the best things in life are free, and this is lucky, because we certainly couldn't afford to buy anything after this project.

Without a shadow of a doubt though, the worst videos to see of your band are those posted online by fans. If you've filmed a show

---

[79] Apart from when I did it again just two years later. Idiot.

yourselves, you then of course get the luxury of going through the footage and choosing only the best song or two to use, perhaps also giving the video and audio a bit of a tweak to improve the quality a little. Too many times I've inadvertently stumbled across a live video posted by a fan to YouTube that hasn't been through our own quality control processes, and it's rarely any fun to watch! Even the best performances are rendered pretty much awful when filmed through a mobile phone[80], but there's nothing you can do about it whatsoever. The only reasonable approach to take is to get one of those Men In Black memory eraser things and forget you ever watched them.

MERCHANDISE

Every band likes the idea of having a stack of merchandise to sell as well as your actual music. Many successful bands will make more money from t-shirts than anything else. You can sell them for a lot more money than a CD, yet unlike the CD you haven't had to spend a fortune making it. You just come up with a design and away you go. If you're getting them made in their thousands then they cost very little per shirt and the profit margins are excellent. But if you're playing little pub gigs a few times a month, then you don't have any money, and to get a batch of decent t-shirts costs a lot of money. Cashflow is king, as ever. Sure, you can pay five bucks a pop for the shirts when you're ordering a thousand of the buggers, but that will take the average pub band a lifetime to sell – if they're lucky. So you try and order fifty instead, and end up paying twenty-five bucks a pop, which is still a very sizable outlay up front. Even if you sell them all with maybe ten bucks profit each, you still need to sell thirty-six of them to break

---

80 I have never done this at a gig, and I'm entirely mystified as to why anyone would ever do this more than once.

even. And after the band have all taken one (or more) as a freebie, breaking even might not be a given. Although it's dead cool to have your own t-shirts, so in the end you think sod it, let's get some done anyway. But what sizes do you get? Probably stick to small, medium and large and just play it safe. And for God's sake, make sure you see a sizing sample before you go ahead. Don't do what we did. I had a drummer who wanted some shirts made and offered to get it all done for us himself to save me the workload. Great I thought, foolishly. I mean how hard can it be? We ended up with fifty shirts that took forever to sell. We had them in a range of sizes from small to extra extra large. However the sizing was so screwed that even the small shirt was too big for me, and I was normally a medium. In reality the sizing we had was large, extra-large, enormous, camping tent, circus tent - and all in a material so thick it would have made moderately effective armour plating. The large sold out in a couple of months, leaving us with a range of tents that we couldn't shift for bloody years. And that was the last time I bothered with t-shirts.

But t-shirts are pretty much the staple merchandise option. If you're Taylor Swift or Ed Sheeran then you can go on tour with a truck full of iPhone covers, jewellery, hoodies, mugs, keyrings, magnets or those stupid beer cosy things, but about the only thing affordable to your average pub band is perhaps some badges or stickers. Naturally you will shop around for the best deal, which translates – incorrectly – as the cheapest deal. We saved a lot of money on five hundred stickers from one particular supplier, with the aim of selling half and plastering the other half all over the city. After a couple of evenings of artistic vandalism spent sticking them in all manner of stupid places we were feeling pretty pleased with ourselves, but after about a week they'd all fallen off. Turns out stickiness, not price, is the key ingredient on your sticker. If only I'd had the chance previously to learn some form of lesson about getting what you pay for.

And then we had the same issue with badges. We got a "great deal" on a thousand small badges which looked brilliant. Sadly only about 1 in 10 seemed to be any good. And the thing with badges is that people want to put one on as soon as they buy one. It got very embarrassing in the end when people would give you a dollar for your badge and then the pin would fall out as soon as they stuck it on. In the end they became "free badge with every CD", but it didn't get any less embarrassing.

Selling your merchandise – and I include CDs in the merchandise category – is vitally important. And an average gig can soon be made to feel like a great one if you manage to sell a whole bunch of merch afterwards! But, like any business, you really need a shop window to showcase your wares, without which it's much harder to sell. The singer announcing "don't forget to come and see us after the show to grab some merch" is not a successful marketing strategy, but sometimes it's all you've got. Some venues simply don't have a handy spot where you can set up an inviting display of items for sale, in which case you have no choice but to stick a bunch of CDs in a bag and wander around the bar hopefully after the gig. But many venues will have a handy spot by the door where you can set up shop. The problem that then arises is who will be shopkeeper? If you're a young band, this is not too tricky, as you'll have any number of hangers-on/girlfriends/boyfriends who you can rope in to do the job – a couple of free drinks is usually enough to seal the deal. Once you're past this stage, things become slightly trickier. If you're very lucky, as I once was for a few years, you'll have someone associated with the band who takes on the job themselves and does it superbly. Spider's girlfriend did this for us, and what a blessed relief it was too. You literally can't buy that sort of assistance. Or rather you could – but not without money. Which you don't have. Like a good roadie, this person becomes an integral part of your organisation and, like a good roadie, you realise just how valuable they are when they're not there and you have to try and do it all yourself. You'll sell most of the merch in perhaps a twenty-minute window that will generally open up towards the end of the show, and close not too long afterwards. Making it a very tricky job to do for someone who is in the band. The drummer won't do it – he takes far longer to pack up his gear than anyone else, on the account of playing the drums. This is no big deal, as most drummers are not the sort of person you want as your shopkeeper. The bassist probably won't do it because for some reason bass players never do this sort of thing. The guitarist will look down their nose at such menial work and, well, what it comes down to is that once again the person who ends up doing it will be the same person that does everything else – because they have the most to gain by doing it and the most to lose by not doing it. And what better way could there be of enjoying yourself post-gig, drenched in sweat, with adrenalin coursing through your veins, than trying to calculate the correct change for someone buying two CDs and a t-shirt and then trying unsuccessfully to find the correct change in your wallet, giving up and then queuing at the bar to try and get the correct change, before returning to your merchandise and finding all the other customers have given up waiting for you and gone home?

Another important tool to keep handy is a supply of pens. People like their CDs signed when they buy them at gigs, which is really quite lovely and makes you feel very special for a few moments. You can attempt to keep a couple of different pens stored with the merchandise for just such occasions, but they will disappear all the time – usually much quicker than the actual merchandise – because that's what pens do. A big thick marker, such as you might use to write out setlists, is no good at all, one needs something a little more delicate. However you also need a couple of options, perhaps a silver or gold pen as well as a black or blue, because you quickly discover that half of your CDs have dark covers that you can't sign with blue or black. The old faithful biro is no good to you either, as they seem to be entirely incapable of working properly on the paper that CD inlays are printed on, and many a CD inlay has been ruined by trying to get them to do so. So it's not simply a case of keeping a good stock of pens at the ready, it's case of keeping a good stock of expensive pens at the ready – you know, the ones much more likely to mysteriously go missing. On a couple of rare occasions at festivals, the band have done pre-arranged signing sessions post-gig, which is much more like it. Festival staff organising tables, chairs, pens and an orderly queue of fans is bloody fantastic and makes you feel like a bona-fida rock star for half an hour, yeah!

On the subject of festivals and merchandise, many festivals will have their own shops for band merch, taking the worry away from the band for the weekend. Some of them do this for free, some of them might take a 10% cut, and I've done a couple where they wanted a mighty 35% of the takings, which seems somewhat excessive. It's always a good idea to check up on them too – I recall one festival shop getting their numbers mixed up and instead of selling our CDs at $20 each, they priced them up at $40. When I went to see how many we'd sold at the end of the festival, it was a predictable none, and their heartfelt apologies were scant consolation. We did one festival that was being run by the local council[81], and you had to sign a contract that stated all merchandise must be sold via official channels, i.e. their little merch tent, and not by yourselves post-show. Not a problem, they were only taking 10%, but it was after the festival that things became tricky. As I talked to them afterwards, I noticed a big box of cash and they showed me a sheet which logged all our CDs that they had sold over the weekend, amounting to about $600. Unsold CDs were duly returned, and I asked – not unreasonably – for the money. *Oh we can't give you the money, you'll have to invoice us for that.* What do you mean, invoice you? You're selling our stock that we gave you, you didn't buy it from us! *That's how it works I'm afraid, send an invoice to the council and they will send you a cheque.* But you have a big box of cash there, from selling our stuff, just hand over the money and we're done! *No, it doesn't work like that. Send an invoice.* If you've ever dealt with a local council for basically anything at all, you'll be well aware that such organisations are usually hives of incompetence and frustration, and so it proved here... nine fucking weeks it took to get that money out of them. Bastards.

THE INTERNET

The internet can probably be best described as a mixed blessing to the musician. Well, to everyone really. People born after about

---

[81] This is not a good sign for anything really, I mean they struggle to collect the bins successfully.

1995 are never going to know a life without it[82] and cannot possibly relate to the notion that just maybe life could be better in some ways without it. These people will never know the joy of not being able to google something immediately to find an answer to a question, and to sometimes not be able to find an answer at all, ever. Imagine a life when the only time you came across a completely offensive prick of a man mouthing off some racist misogynistic nonsense in a barely intelligible language was as you walked past him on the way home from the pub after closing[83], rather than on every second page of the internet. People had to write books about being in bands without checking in on Twitter every ten minutes. It simply doesn't bear thinking about.

I think it was probably around about 2002 that the net became a seriously useful promotional tool for a band. Indeed, for a short period[84], you could be ahead of the curve and get your band an online presence while it was something of a novelty, before you were lost in the crowd of other bands all clawing for the attention of the potential fans eagerly surfing this new-fangled internet thing[85]. Like-minded people mutually linked their home-made band websites to those of their friends' bands, and people might just stumble across your band this way. Decent streaming of music was way off, but you could download an mp3 of an average length song on a dial-up connection in about a quarter of an hour. While that wasn't of much interest to

---

82 Not until the apocalypse anyway.

83 Or on prime-time Australian television.

84 This now legendary window was open for precisely 26 minutes, a brief space that opened up after enough people had decent web access and before web pages sprung up for every known band since the dawn of time.

85 Although now that every band and their dog could release their music online you had about as much chance of being discovered by chance as you had of somebody finding your CD in a record store the size of Greater London.

the passer-by, it still became a decent option in your promotional artillery. You could put them on your website for fans or bookers to download. This was much more cost effective than constantly mailing CDs all over the world (although I suspect back then that the CD was far more likely to get a listen). In the days before social media, bands had websites that people actually visited, websites that weren't simply portals to iTunes, Instagram and Facebook pages, and the variety in designs and ideas were actually pretty cool. There were numerous good gig-guide websites where you could promote shows too. Social media's subsequent takeover of everything on the net was akin to the shopping malls and chain stores taking over the town – although it happened much quicker.

Even early social media however was a really cool thing for a band. When Myspace sprung up and became the hip place to hang out between about 2004-2009, it had a real sense of community about it, and was of course something entirely new. As a fan you could make friends with bands, you may even feature on the band's top eight friends! You could crash your computer by inadvertently dropping in on a page designed by some complete arse of a human who had loaded so much content onto their page that your internet connection simply couldn't cope, and neither could your eyes. As a band you could take gushing praise[86] and vitriolic abuse[87] from a whole new range of people all over the world. Cross-pollination was everywhere and searching out like-minded souls was a great thing - Myspace allowed you to search for bands by area and by musical influences, and this was a tool I used to great effect, finding like-minded bands

---
86 So I'm told.
87 Without a doubt.

in other cities to get gigs with.

Facebook came along and started eroding the Myspace market share after a few years, the main point of difference perhaps being a newsfeed timeline that enabled you to get a rolling feed of updates from any pages you liked or friends you had made. This was a great idea and bands soon jumped on it, quickly realising its potential for marketing gigs. Facebook of course had already realised that potential, but happily sat back[88] while bands made the most of it. People are at heart lazy creatures who really love convenience, so to be able to "like" all your favourite bands on Facebook and then get a post in your feed when a new release or tour was happening was far simpler than having to keep visiting a band's website, or subscribing to yet another email newsletter. As a result, bands started to concentrate their energies onto enlarging their following on Facebook, encouraging people to like them, entering into conversations with them as well as simply promoting stuff. And ye olde band website became a rather forlorn middle-aged dude at the back of the room that nobody paid any attention to anymore, even though he was quite interesting, standing under a broken light bulb and remembering the glory of his youth when all these other people here thought he was pretty damn groovy actually. In fact the only person that even acknowledged this dude now was the email newsletter, a tired looking chick who, while never being half as cool as this guy, had been reliable and fun, before the constant strain of rejection by security staff had led to her becoming something of a recluse who now rarely went out at all cos like what was the point y'know?

---

88 Presumably in a swivel chair, with an evil grin on their face, stroking a white cat.

There was a period for a year or two when Facebook was pretty much the only promotional tool worth using for your band. Heaps of your fans were there, post-sharing was rife and if you played your cards right the fans would basically end up doing the promotion for you. Then, once Facebook realised that phase one of their plans for world domination were complete, they enacted phase two. New algorithms were aimed and launched, ready to obliterate their targets and we all expressed indignant surprise that a large corporation's primary motive wasn't providing us with a handy tool for no charge but rather was to make money for itself. Suddenly your posts were being shown to 100 people instead of 1000, but hey you can increase the visibility of your post by paying to reach these people instead, isn't that great? Instead of logging in to find a flurry of notifications from fans commenting on your latest tour snaps, you could experience the joy of logging in and finding a flurry of notifications from Facebook telling you that your latest post was receiving more views than ninety percent of your other similar posts so why not pay to extend that reach further? We'd been totally had, naively falling for an epic scam, and now it was too late to do anything about it. Practically all other online outlets had been neglected or discarded in favour of Facebook, and now it was next to useless unless you paid for it, which was of course the exact opposite of the reason you started using it originally. Every band I know has opted at some stage to try the "sponsored post", but I don't know any that have done it more than once. I'm not even convinced the sponsored post reached more users than normal, but I do know it would appear multiple times on the same people's newsfeed, to the point of genuine irritation. Meanwhile, internet users' habits are now so ingrained that nobody bothers straying far from their social media accounts, and email – outside of business – has almost become a thing of the past. Basically Facebook invited us all into their fancy mansion, showed us a good time, knocked down our own houses while we were enjoying theirs, and then told us to pay up or they'd kick us out onto the street. The bastards!

YouTube grew quickly into an enormous monster of a website, of which now at least 95% of the content is utter rubbish[89]. I suspect it's probably become the number one method of checking out a band, along with Spotify perhaps. Before the internet it was hardly worth making a video for your song because there was almost nobody who would broadcast an independent video. With the advent of YouTube, all of a sudden you could publish a video yourself and it became a fantastic way to promote your song. I think your average punter is more likely to engage with something new that they can both listen to *and* watch – even though more often than not the visual aspect distracts one from the music. It has now reached the stage where you can't really release a song without an accompanying video, which invariably takes more effort to produce than the song itself and requires an entirely different skill set. For people who book bands, YouTube must be fantastic – you can see what a band looks like and sounds like live. Well, sort of. You get an idea at least. From the band's point of view it's perhaps not ideal... getting a live performance captured on video that looks and sounds great is no mean feat and to do it properly costs a lot of money. There is perhaps no better way of making a great band appear shit than seeing them via a live video recorded on someone's phone and posted on YouTube. YouTube themselves don't help matters – once you upload even your pristine new high-definition video clip, the YouTube machine goes into action

---

89 In fairness, this is no different to television, and unlike television YouTube achieved this without any quality control whatsoever.

and starts compressing everything with incredible enthusiasm, and within a minute or two both the audio and video files have been crushed so hard that you begin to wonder why you didn't just record the song and the film clip directly to your phone in the first place instead of relying on outmoded concepts such as recording studios and camera crews.

For a while iPods and iTunes seemed set to take over the world, and people everywhere were ditching their CDs, just as they'd previously ditched their vinyl[90], in favour of mp3 files. The convenience of the mp3 was undeniable, although the potential to lose your entire music collection in one hard drive crash was also undeniable, and I know many people who suffered this. But from the point of view of being in an independent band, it was again a mixed blessing. On the plus side, releasing an album digitally is much cheaper than manufacturing a run of CDs, but you sell most of your CDs at gigs – and you can't sell downloads at gigs. It's far, far easier to get a punter to buy something at a show than it is to get them to buy something online a few days or weeks after the gig. When they're actually there with a drink or two inside them, having just enjoyed a good set of live music, with the opportunity to now meet the band and perhaps get their purchase signed, then it's much easier to get them to part with some cash. But people's buying habits were changing quickly, especially amongst the younger generation. Up until about 2013, we'd find that we'd play a festival on a weekend and bank on selling $500-$1000 worth of CDs. Over the next couple of years, despite playing better shows to bigger crowds, the CD revenue dropped down to $200-$300. The knock-on

---

[90] Which they now enjoy buying back at grossly inflated prices. Now is probably a good time to start buying second-hand CDs.

effect of this meant that you had to start producing less CDs, so you might do a run of 100 instead of 500 before a tour, thus the price per unit went up accordingly. Not only were you selling less CDs, but the profit margin was cut in half as well. Still, you'd make up at least some[91] of the money with revenue from iTunes or perhaps an independent site like Bandcamp[92].

And then along came streaming, and the download money dropped away in the same way as the CD money did. Again, the potential audience is enormous when your music is available on Spotify, as it was with iTunes, but the reality is that you're just another band most people have never heard off and you simply drown in the vast sea of music that these sites contain. I reckon over the last ten years the amount of music I've sold has probably remained fairly constant from year to year, but as the technology changed and the market went from CDs to downloads to streaming, the actual revenue simply dropped over a cliff.

There are plenty of great things about using the internet to promote your band, and plenty of... not so great things. Undoubtedly the worst thing is the sheer amount of time it can consume. Even for an independent self-managed band with a small following, there is easily enough to do to merit employing a full time person to do it for you – well, there would be if there was any money to be made, which of course there isn't. In fact, there's far more work to be done for the independent artist than the successful international rock star.

---

91 5% still qualifies as "some", right?
92 Lower profile than iTunes, but you don't lose a third of your income to the distributor or have to pay a fee to create the new release.

If you're Halsey then all you have to do is knock out a quick post on Twitter and Instagram with a release date for a new song, and within ten minutes it's been shared all over the world by millions and millions of fans. Job done. You don't need to worry about posting or hosting your own videos or photos because there will be loads of fans and tribute pages that are doing that for you. But for the unsigned underground band trying to get someone – anyone – to notice them, there is no end to the amount of websites you could create accounts for to host songs, videos, photos, advertise gigs etc. And the more of these sites that you sign up for and create accounts with for your band, the more you have to keep track of, the more you have to keep updated. The thing about doing this is that most of the time you can't help yourself, even though you know you are wasting your time and that the only people visiting these websites are the bands themselves. But you do it anyway, just in case. And you do it yourself, because, as we've seen previously, the saying "if you want something doing properly, do it yourself" is always correct (except when it's not). Many of these sites will offer "premium services" in an attempt to milk you for whatever money you have left – priority placements on the site for your band, "professional" feedback for your latest song and other such nonsense. This is of course the real reason the website exists in the first place, to prey on the endless supply of ever-hopeful young bands still foolish enough to fall for such scams.

As a footnote to this section, I'd like to add that one of the curious things about the internet was that it showed just how little people cared about audio quality, and how much more people care about convenience. At the same time as video quality just kept getting better and better – from DVD to full HD technology - audio just kept getting worse. First CDs gave way to mp3 files that were notably inferior in terms of sound quality, and then dedicated hi-fi systems became pretty much redundant as people started storing mp3s first on iPods and then later simply streaming them on smartphones through crappy ear buds or Bluetooth speakers. I'm guilty of doing the same in fairness, but if I've enjoyed streaming an album I'll usually buy the CD, and there is a real joy in hearing the CD version through a decent set of speakers. I mourn the apparent lack of appreciation for audio quality, while also being vaguely aware that I've probably turned into an old man yelling at cloud meme. Oh well.

TV, RADIO & PRINT

I remember the first time that an article about my band appeared in print, and it was *incredibly* exciting. A review of your band's new demo in the local newspaper might not be much in the overall scheme of things, but it's an ever-so-slight taste of the fame you're hungering after, and as – in this case – the review was a good one, it was something to be proud of for both the band *and* your parents. I still have a copy of said review, and while it's written in that sort of slightly patronising yet enthusiastic style that local newspapers excel at, the fact that it compared me to David Bowie leads me to think that in retrospect it was also probably the best review I ever had. The town's local rag had a regular live music section, featuring reviews, interviews and gig listings. I don't know if there are still local papers that do this – perhaps there are, but every one I've picked up in the last decade or so has basically been twenty pages of real estate advertisement, and perhaps some local classified ads for plumbers, dog walkers, and massages with happy endings. The thing about local newspapers though is that, for all their shortcomings, they are often desperate for any vaguely interesting local content and the journalists are usually young and sweetly keen, not yet burdened with the awful cynicism that decades of experience brings[93]. So for the independent band scratching around for any sort of publicity, they are well worth bearing in mind. And the great thing about them is that when they make an absolute mess of an article about you, you can rest easy knowing that nobody will ever read it anyway. I've done a number of interviews with an assortment of local papers over the years, and most of them have been mildly embarrassing, if only because the journalists are not music journalists and often don't have the faintest idea what you or indeed themselves are talking about. It doesn't matter how cool you sounded – or thought you sounded – during the interview, the Smalltown Herald can and will reduce you to sounding like a bit of a twat by misquoting you horrendously and creating a headline for the article which you can be absolutely sure will include a really bad pun. I once did an interview that I thought went really well – I got on with the journalist, had a bit of a laugh and looked forward to the article. I knew it would at least be done with some care and attention because the journalist in question was a good friend of one of my bandmates, and as we had a few gigs in the area coming up I thought this one might actually have some value. When it finally appeared, the writer had managed to get both my first name *and* my surname wrong[94], printed the wrong tour dates and misspelt the band name. In addition to this, the quotes attributed to me were so badly mangled that only the presence of my photo convinced me that yes, this was about me.

---

93 Unlike me.
94 Right number of characters in both names, but entirely the wrong letters.

Mind you, being badly misquoted is something that has happened with pretty much every interview I've ever done that I've seen in print, and it would be unfair to suggest it only happens with the Smalltown Herald. I can only imagine how utterly infuriating it must be to an artist that promotes their new tour or album with hundreds of interviews to major publications read by thousands or even millions of people. I understand of course that a certain amount of editing and paraphrasing has to happen when a journalist puts an article together, but it's amazing how many writers seem to ignore what you do say, and instead write what they think you said while they weren't really listening. Luckily if you're me and nobody is reading it then it doesn't really matter, but when Rolling Stone has just pretty much fabricated your views on a number of contentious subjects, it must be a little vexing to say the least. I can totally understand artists that just reach a point where they say fuck it, I'm not doing interviews anymore, which of course means that they then get articles written about how up themselves they are and how they're not willing to talk to their fans now they're too famous.

In the nineties there were still quite a lot of fanzines being made. I've got a lot of time for the humble fanzine – despite the invariably dodgy production values, usually the unavoidable consequence of being done with even less money than a band has, they were always made with much love and a commendable degree of enthusiasm *and* knowledge of their subject matter. The circulation was usually tiny, perhaps a few copies distributed in the local record shops, but in my experience they punched far above their weight in terms of content quality. I wrote for a friend's fanzine for a little while, and it was very enjoyable – I particularly appreciated the large volumes of free albums that started coming my way, although I gave up after getting the chance to interview one of my musical heroes at the time, who turned out to be a right arse. I totally understand that being interviewed by a teenage nobody for a crappy fanzine before your gig is not exactly the highlight of your day, but you could at least make *some* effort to not be a cunt about it. Or maybe I deserved it. Anyway, I still see the odd fanzine around on the rare occasions I visit an actual record shop, but most of these sort of publications migrated to the internet. For a while I spent a fair bit of time keeping an eye on some of the thousands of independent blogs that reviewed music from time to time, but none of the websites ever seemed to capture the essence of the old-fashioned fanzine.

When I was finding my feet in my early bands in England, there was the aforementioned local paper and the odd fanzine, followed by a quantum leap to the national publications – weekly magazines such as the New Musical Express and Melody Maker, or the monthly publications such as Q or Select. For the most part you stood absolutely no chance of featuring in one of the glossy monthlies, and only a slightly better chance of featuring in one of the weeklies[95]. Melody Maker used to do a little half page section where they'd review demos from independent bands, and one of my bands did manage to get a surprise mention one week in this category – unfortunately the rather unflattering review appeared some eighteen months after the demo had been submitted, and in the meantime we'd found our feet and our sound, and released a couple of singles. So instead of all your

---

95 Unless you were playing the right gigs in Camden Town and buying enough drink and drugs for the right journalist, in which case you could conceivably go from nowhere to featuring on the NME cover for two weeks in a row, before you became yesterday's news in week three as you were no longer in fashion.

mates saying "hey good work guys, saw you in Melody Maker this week!", all our mates were saying "hey guys, why are Melody Maker reviewing that crappy old demo of yours from a couple of years back this week?".

However, when I arrived in Australia I discovered something called the Street Press. This was hugely impressive to me at first – free weekly magazines with features and reviews of both gigs and new releases. All the venues, shops and studios would advertise as well, so it was a handy directory of the local music scene. You could pick them up every week from pretty much anywhere, surely this was the perfect way to get your band noticed? Well, it was. And also it wasn't. Despite submitting numerous press releases and CDs over the years, I never managed to get a mention beyond the local band news at the back – basically a sentence or two about your news that you could submit to the magazine, that they would then print if they felt like it, more often than not adding a few typos in for good measure. I could never quite get my head around the utter lack of support that my band (or indeed any of my friend's bands) received from these publications. And then slowly it dawned on me that the bands that featured in the full colour double page spreads, the bands that got their albums and their gigs reviewed, were exactly the same bands that had advertisements in that issue. In a variation of the pay-to-play approach so much loved by venues in London, the street press would happily give you a good review if you advertised with them[96]. The more you paid for your advert, the more coverage you would get. The simple economics of producing a free magazine each week means that, as with the local newspaper, advertising revenue is king, so I

---

96 They were of course always good reviews – I mean who is going to pay for a bad review?

fully appreciate the reasons for doing it this way, but it does rather undercut any claim to any form of editorial credibility whatsoever. I duly paid up for a few adverts over the years, and although it never made the blindest bit of difference to audience numbers, I guess – like with poster campaigns – that there was probably some value as a branding exercise. But when they finally wrote an article or review about my band, it was always a half-arsed cut and paste job from our press releases, with additional typos and factual errors thrown in as freebies. Presumably if I'd managed to afford a full-page rather than a quarter-page advert then more attention would have been paid to the writing, but even a quarter-page advert meant that you'd just guaranteed a loss on the gig you were advertising. Another favourite technique of one particular magazine was to take your advertising money with the promise of an article, which they would then run the week *after* your advert, when the gig was done and dusted. An original and unusual approach for sure, but rather infuriating and one that I haven't seen catch on anywhere else in the media industry.

There was one monthly magazine in Australia that took the pay-to-feature approach to a new level. I paid for an advert for a new album which came with the guarantee of a full in-depth article about the band, as well as a review of the album. The review was very good – by which I mean it was written entirely by someone who had actually listened to the album[97], rather than someone cutting and pasting the press release I'd submitted with the CD. The article/interview that also appeared that issue was glowing, and every single quote from myself was perfectly reproduced. It remains by some distance the best article I have ever seen about my band, in fact I'd go as far

---

97   I know, amazing right?! Apparently this is called journalism.

as to say that it was exactly how I'd have written it myself. This was due to the fact that I had in fact written it myself. By outsourcing their journalism to the advertiser, the magazine saved themselves wages and guaranteed the customer satisfaction of said advertiser. The absurdity of this was only increased when I realised that I could now quote this article's glowing praise of my band on future press releases[98]. Something about this seems more than a little wrong, but I have a suspicion that it's probably par for the course for most newspapers these days as well and who am I to judge?

Growing up in small town England meant that my options when it came to radio that played contemporary music were fairly limited. Limited to one, in fact. BBC Radio One, which was for the most part a little on the excruciating side. Even listening to genuinely entertaining DJs such as Mark Radcliffe and, well, that was about it really, was quite painful due to the corporate pop music that made up most of the playlist. There was of course the legendary John Peel, who somehow survived on the station as the sole purveyor of independent and perhaps unsigned artists, although generally in some pretty unfriendly time slots. I never really got into Peel's shows, principally because I can't stand The Fall or The Undertones, but he is rightly considered an absolute legend. Nevertheless, you didn't stand much chance of getting some nationwide airplay on Radio 1 by sending in your new demo, which left your local radio station. Every county had a local station or two, and despite the fact that this allows for potentially hundreds of different stations, they were all exactly the same, and as far as I can remember they all had exactly the same playlists, a mixture of about twenty new pop singles and

---

98 Although it's a hollow feeling.

twenty classics by Phil Collins, Dire Straits, Queen, Sting and Elton John, which would be repeated day in day out on every single show, interspersed with hilariously bad adverts for local businesses, and the latest local traffic bulletins. You *could* get your new single played on these stations, but only if you disguised it as Easy Lover by Phil Collins and they played it by accident. I did once get interviewed on our local station in the lead up to a big show we were doing that weekend, and you would think that this would at least get us some airplay, but no, we chatted for ten minutes and then they played Angels by Robbie Williams. I think there were actually some decent independent radio stations in London at the time, but you couldn't pick them up where I lived, and this meant in the pre-internet era that you were entirely unaware of them.

There was a good deal of excitement in the early nineties when we discovered that the nearby town of Milton Keynes had a cable radio station. My understanding of cable radio stations is that they were just like FM radio stations, except nobody listened to them because you couldn't receive them on an actual radio. We sent them a demo, which they said they played, and we took their word for it because like everybody else who didn't live within a couple of miles of central Milton Keynes with a television set tuned into the radio station, we couldn't actually listen to it. But they clearly enjoyed it, as they invited us in to do a live session. Awesome! This was a seriously big deal as you can imagine, our first radio session – suddenly we had an extra spring in our step and an extra layer of credibility added to the band. It is worth pointing out at this time that the demo they'd received (the same one that got the great review in the local paper and compared us to Bowie) was a predominantly laid-back acoustic affair that might sit happily alongside some Simon and Garfunkel. Since the recording however, the band had evolved and added a bit more grit, recruiting a drummer whose favourite band was Lawnmower Deth and replacing our acoustic guitarist with a friend of mine on electric guitar whose sole aim was to mimic his hero wherever possible - Dave Murray from Iron Maiden. As we lugged the 12-piece drum kit and the Marshall stack into the rather cosy studio, we began to pick up a slight um-this-is-not-at-all-what-we-were-expecting kind of vibe, which developed into a full what-the-fuck-is-happening-here-argh-my-ears-my-ears kind of vibe when we began to play. There was no soundcheck – we just launched straight into a five-song set of blisteringly loud new wave rock'n'roll, live-to-air![99] We finished up and the only comment from the DJ was "well that was, um... raw... thanks guys". Good fun though.

In the late nineties, prior to relocating to Australia, I spent a year or so living in New Zealand, where I discovered Auckland's magical independent radio station, 95bFM. Unlike England, where the radio stations had such imaginative taglines as "Chiltern FM – serving the Chilterns and the Aylesbury Vale" or "Cotswold Radio – radio for the Cotswolds", bFM's tagline was "95bFM – other radio stations are shit". Naturally this instantly sold the station to me, and I tuned in every day to hear a massive range of new music, no programmed commercial playlists whatsoever, a full range of colourful language and, hell, even the adverts were funny. This was radio as it should be. I expected something similar when I moved to Australia, and while there were some stations operating under a similar model, none of them were anywhere near as good – or as funny – as Radio B. However, living in

---

99 Is it still air? Live to cable, perhaps?

Melbourne gave you a handful of community radio stations that were only too happy to play your independent releases, on the proviso that you were mates with the DJ or were paying for advertising. Actually, that's a little unfair... there were many times that I had songs played on these stations, rarely a high profile show, but beggars can't be choosers and any airplay is good airplay! Unfortunately beggars also can't afford to pay for advertising. We approached a radio station to drop off some advance copies of our new album and find out how we could perhaps get a live session happening to link in with our album launch and subsequent tour, and perhaps some airplay for the album in the week leading up to it. Despite all the monumental evidence I had accumulated to the contrary over my lifetime, I still had a notion that you could get picked up on by the media purely because someone in the right place really liked your music. And perhaps that does happen, and perhaps my bands have just all been too sub-standard to merit any form of exposure[100], but everything points rather firmly in the direction of this notion being entirely misguided. I never saw anything in my dealings with these radio stations to suggest they were quite as cynical about the process as the street press were, and they were always very nice people doing what they had to do to keep their poorly paid jobs that they clearly loved - but it's a tough thing for any artist to be told that the only way we're going to push your art is if you give us money. Even if it's shit, we'll push it for you if you pay us. We agreed to pay for an advert for our tour in exchange for a live session and an on-air interview, but we were unable to stump up the cash for the next level of exposure which would have meant regular primetime airplay throughout the week and the possibility of being considered for album of the week. Ironically the advert we paid for

---

[100] I am entirely ready to believe this is the case, but having seen the same thing happen to countless bands I've known over the decades that were far better than mine, I suspect this is in fact not the case.

was promoting three gigs in the general locality over the weekend, two of which were bloody cancelled at the last minute, the remaining show being at a venue that paid us a set fee regardless of how many people showed up! Still, the live session was a real blast and we sold a few albums on the back of it, so at least it felt like we got some value out of the whole thing.

Radio exposure has always been of huge value, but the real gold is television. Or was. I don't really know now – the explosion of TV channels and streaming services has changed the landscape beyond all recognition in a very short period. For a few years in the mid-noughties there was a late-night weekend show in Australia on one of the two publicly owned stations that played video clips by independent bands, and they hooked onto one of our clips and played it month after month, which had a big impact on our profile amongst all the stoners that were still awake and watching television at 2am. We didn't even have to pay them! Although now that I think about it, maybe we did – I wrote and recorded a new theme tune for the show, thirty seconds of music for the opening credits, and I never received any royalties. I've only just realised this. Still, a worthwhile trade, on balance. They also had their own venue that they operated the studio from, where they'd film live acts every week and do the occasional interview. Sadly their production values and quality control left a little bit to be desired at times and the show was dropped, which was a real bummer. There were a couple of other shows at the time that operated along similar lines but broadcast on a Melbourne-only TV station. One of these had a wonderfully professional set up with good lighting, great sound rig and personnel who really knew their stuff. They operated out of a live venue and recording studio complex

– you could get a gig there and they'd film the set and broadcast a couple of songs a few weeks later. Everything about this setup was excellent, except for the location. Based on an industrial estate in the grim outer suburbs of the city, with no public transport access or indeed available parking, getting people to come along was a bloody nightmare. So you got a great quality film of your band playing on TV - to an audience of about eight people. The other show of a similar ilk on the channel was a different kettle of fish entirely. Based in the city, you'd play a show to a sizeable and colourful audience and the attention to detail was impressive – great camerawork, good lighting, nice tv studio, and they even had a make-up team to bring out the best in your appearance! Sadly it seemed that nobody was involved that really grasped live music, so there was no monitoring for the bands. What this means is that while performing you can of course hear the drummer (hearing a drummer is very rarely a problem as you can imagine) and also the rest of the band via their amplifiers. But the microphones for the singers just went straight into the recording console and to a small speaker near the audience. Even at the worst gigs in the worst pubs, you'll be able to hear at least some of the vocals on stage via the PA speakers, and most venues will have some form of monitors (i.e. the wedge-shaped speakers at the front of the stage that point back at the band so they can actually hear themselves, especially vital for the vocalist). But in this case, I simply sang into a microphone unable to hear my voice at all and basically just hoping for the best. This is not a recipe for a great vocal performance, and not the way you want to sell yourself on television. Not for the first time I found myself falling back on the consolation that there was probably nobody watching or listening anyway.

THE ALBUM LAUNCH

A new album is always the best excuse for a gig or a tour, and it makes sense to push these gigs with extra promotion. It's generally your best chance of getting a decent crowd and selling a bunch of CDs. Venues or festivals will look favourably on an album launch show, presuming[101] that they will attract a bigger crowd than a "normal"[102] show. The problem from a band's point of view is that the release of an album is always the time when you are even more broke than normal. Because, and this is the catch 22 you find yourself in, you've just recorded an album. You have no money left. In fact the best time to promote a show, from the bands point of view, is when you've just finished a tour and haven't been in the studio for a year or two - because you might actually have some cash available at this point. Obviously from an artistic point of view you want to produce as good an album as you possibly can, but the reality is that you're probably[103] better off spending less money on the recording and spending it on promotions instead. I once spent the best part of $15,000 recording an album, and when I came to release it I had about $200 left with which to promote it. What I should have done, perhaps, was to spend $5,000 recording the album and then $10,000 promoting it. This would have enabled me to spend a few grand on a publicist to actually publicise the damn thing, and a few grand on advertising on the radio and street press all over the country. God, imagine how much airplay we could have bought with that! Even though the quality of the recording would have been lower, it would have still

---

101 Often wrongly.
102 Of course, most successful bands are always playing shows in support of a new release. That's what they do – release something, tour it. But for us less successful bands, shows are booked whenever possible, in the name of getting exposure, a bit of cash and just for the thrill of playing.
103 Definitely.

been good enough. But the advertising would have gone from non-existent to very well-funded, quite possibly enough to make a quite different career path appear. But while a musician is happy to dish out ridiculous sums of money on instruments, studios and possibly drugs, I have never met one who is entirely happy about spending large sums on something as grotesque as advertising. And that, dear reader, is why I still have about 50 copies of that $15,000 album in a box under the desk in my studio fifteen years later.

11.
PLAYING LIVE

Nothing beats playing gigs. Well, nothing beats playing good gigs anyway. Shit gigs are a truly awful experience, but I guess that's the Yin and the Yang of the whole experience or something.

The very first gig I did was with the first band I'd had that was *my* band doing *my* songs, rather than a bunch of us getting together and knocking out covers of each other's favourite tunes. Well, I say band, it was just two of us – acoustic guitar and bass. It was in a hugely unimpressive back room of a pub in a town 45 minutes away from where I lived, which was just far enough away to discourage any friends from coming. We were supporting a band made up of some friends of Den, the bass player. Curiously I don't recall much in the way of nerves, despite this being the first time I'd sung in public, and this would make sense – time has long ago proven that I was born to play in hugely unimpressive back rooms of pubs. I was simply fulfilling my destiny. Anyway, the gig was quite enjoyable, in large part because of the relief of having finally done it. But the reaction of the perhaps thirty people[104] in the room was positive enough and nobody had thrown anything. We were awful of course, but not

---
104 Don't laugh. Thirty people is great!

awful enough that people felt the need to go and stand outside. The band we were supporting, also doing their first gig, were a different proposition. What they had going for them compared to us, was a drummer and a very good bass player. Going against them was having a singer/guitarist who couldn't sing and who played very badly at an absolutely ear-bleeding volume. It wasn't long before all the people felt the need to go and stand outside. Even though they were friends of the band and it was starting to rain. The drummer Trevor was a good laugh though, and it turned out he lived in the same town as me, so I poached him for my band. All in all a good night.

As you start playing your first shows, your experience increases at a fierce rate, one that barely lets up until you retire, or die. You learn to deal with a wide range of varied situations, many that will crop up again and again, and many that are strict one-offs. There is no such thing as having seen it all before. Seen nearly everything, sure, but seen it all? No. Gigs never quite lose their ability to surprise. Like the time some guy came up to me post show and told me he loved us so much that he was going to take off all his clothes in honour of the gig, which he proceeded to do, and stood there looking very proud of himself, in more ways than one. Never did I envisage that happening, but thankfully it was a strict one-off. So to speak.

Anyway, one lesson you will learn repeatedly early on is that there are always better bands than you, and it's no fun when you have to follow them onstage. One genuinely horrible gig my first band did was perhaps the fourth or fifth that we played, and only the second time we were heading out of our home town to play. The venue had put on a support band for us which we knew wouldn't be a patch on our own brand of slightly fey punkish indie pop. Something was amiss from the start - as I walked into the pub wearing my fur coat[105] and my eyeliner only to find it full of scary-looking leather-clad tattooed bikers, I felt the sort of glare you get from a scary-looking leather-clad tattooed gang of bikers when you walk into their pub wearing a fur coat and eyeliner. A voice inside me was beginning to chirp up, voicing some possible reservations about the night to come, but I was sure we'd win over any crowd with our fresh and edgy brilliance. We set up and sound-checked, a slightly depressing affair as we struggled to get the vocals anywhere approaching an audible level in the mix. After resigning ourselves to the fact that the PA was crap, we went and sat back to watch the very grizzled-looking support band set up. Again, the voice inside me chirped up, pointing out that these guys in the support band are all part of the biker gang, and are in fact playing to all their mates in their local pub. As they started their set, it became clear that not only are they playing to their mates in their local, they're playing the favourite songs of all their mates too. As the pub pumped to the sound of well-rehearsed rockers playing bang-on versions of songs like Free's Alright Now, the Stones's Satisfaction, Motorhead's Ace of Spades and other rock classics - the singer having no problems at all with the PA as he's got a voice like Freddie Mercury - the voice inside suggested that it was out of here and I was now very much on my own on this one. Honestly, you could have actually brought in Motorhead that night, and they couldn't have gone down any better than our support act did. Although they'd have done a much better job of following them. As they came offstage, the friendly singer gave me a wink and a punch on the arm and said there ya go son, got 'em all warmed up for ya. I

---

105 Fake, naturally.

briefly got my hopes up when I saw that a few car-loads of our friends had turned up, so we'd have some support after all, and this may not be such a bad night - in fact this could be fantastic! In fact, it wasn't. It was even worse than I had feared. We finished the first song, and I suffered through the split-second of not knowing what the reaction is going to be[106], before arriving at the point of the reaction itself, or in this case the point of no reaction. A pub full of bikers stared at us in silence, arms folded, with a collective expression suggesting that if we were going to make them suffer with another fifty-seven minutes of this shit, they were going to make us suffer too. The vibe was strong enough to subdue all our own friends – who were all seated right in the middle of the room in front of the stage – into complete silence. They were all so nervous of the pub regulars that not one of them could muster up the courage to do anything other than sit in silence. And just to rub it in, they left in small groups over the course of our set, so that by the time we finished, all of them had gone. We played our whole set and got nothing more than a stare from anyone[107]. I think this was the first time, but certainly not the last, that I found myself wishing I could put on a magical ring and simply disappear à la Bilbo Baggins. It's always worse for the singer too, being as you are the natural focal point for people watching, and the one charged with coaxing something from the crowd, perhaps breaking the ice with a witty refrain. Not for the singer the option of adjusting his cymbals so nobody can see his face, or the possibility of staring at your feet for the whole show. These sort of experiences are of course character building, and you learn far more from a bad gig than a good gig – in this case the main takeout from the night was Trevor, don't you ever book us a gig there again you bastard. Still, while there are always

---

106 Still hopeful for one last brief moment that this will be a great gig.
107 This has since happened on numerous occasions in fact, but normally it's a stare of apathy, rather than a stare of threat.

bands better than you, there are also lots of bands worse than you, which is always a comforting thought to hold onto.

The audience reaction is crucial to every gig. The band feeds off the energy from a crowd that's enjoying itself, and that energy feeds back into the performance, and a gig will go from good to great. Likewise, the energy from a crowd that's not enjoying itself will also feed into the band's performance, and a gig will go from bad to worse. And there often seems no rhyme nor reason to audience reaction. It just is. Remember, we're not talking about playing gigs to a crowd of two thousand people, most of which own at least some of your albums and whom have all willingly paid money to specifically come and watch you play. Rather we're talking about playing gigs to twenty-five people who have never heard of you and who are frankly pissed off that the tv has been turned off because the band is starting, or playing gigs to one drunk, his dog and a barmaid, or playing gigs to fifty people at a wedding, or playing gigs at far-off country festivals to audiences that are not at all comfortable with the fact that your band are not dressed in jeans and t-shirts and may well actually be – urgh – city folk. Although it's hard to predict the sort of audience and reaction you will get before you arrive at the venue, I find it is surprisingly easy to predict it once you're there. There's something in the air when it's going to be a good gig, and you pick up on that – some intangible buzz about the place. And likewise, when it's destined to be a poor night, I can tell from pretty much the moment I walk in the venue. There's a familiar air of apathy, a dismal lack of life in the ether that the senses pick up on immediately. You then go through the motions of getting ready, already suspecting a dismal crowd or bad performance, but hoping that just maybe something will change, and the night will come good. And it's the hope that kills you.

Sometimes you'll get a pleasant surprise though. One of the most memorable shows I played was in Camden Town in London. We were the first band of the night, and as we readied ourselves to go on it was rather depressing to note that the room had three people in it – two friends that had travelled down to see us, and the soundman. Oh well, may as well have some fun anyway, at least we're playing a fashionable London venue! We kicked off our set, and by the end of the first song people started pouring in from the bar downstairs. As we slammed into our second number, much to our surprise the people just kept coming and five minutes after we'd begun our set to three people, we were now playing to a packed room of about 200 punters who were going crazy for us. None of these people had ever heard us before – we're in the pre-internet era here – and to this day I still feel a curious sense of both pride and bafflement when I think about this gig. The Universe decided in its ineffable wisdom that we seemed to be having too much of a good thing though, and chose to bring us down to earth by having our bass player inexplicably losing his shit at the end of our set and smashing his guitar to pieces. Yeah, way to spoil the mood, dude.

Mind you, sometimes you can get a great audience reaction, and then inadvertently kill it yourself. I was doing a tour of England with a stripped back version of my Australian band,[108] and having a fine

---

108 Basically saving money and hassle by leaving the unnecessary baggage at home - amps, pedal boards, bassist, drummer.

old time. After a show in Somerset we were invited back from the pub to a party in a big old barn – play another set for them at the barn and they'd keep the beer and food coming for us all night. This was a deal we were more than happy with, especially given that the other option was to return to our run-down Travelodge Hotel. There were considerably more people at the barn than at the pub, and we were going down a storm. Until, that is, my decision to play a song we'd played a couple of times on the tour to much acclaim, a song that tore into the former British Prime Minister Margaret Thatcher. This was a critical misreading of my audience, who were deep inside the Tory heartland of England and regarded Maggie as something of a hero. Despite only minimal booing and swearing from the crowd, the disapproving looks were everywhere, and they decided to ignore us from then on. Within five minutes of this, we'd packed up and left, with barely a thank you and certainly no more beer. In my defence, they'd really enjoyed that song in Hull and Sheffield.

Then there are the gigs when you get no reaction. Literally nothing. This is possibly even more soul-destroying than a poor reaction. These are the shows where you are simply background music. Anyone who has done enough shows will have encountered this at some point. These are generally shows at a café or restaurant perhaps, an establishment that will advertise live music but is most definitely not a music venue, if that makes any sense. There are plenty of musicians for whom such shows are their bread and butter – perhaps an acoustic duo performing cover versions, a string quartet or a very safe jazz band. You can earn money doing this sort of thing if you're prepared to accept such a miserable thrill-less existence, but it's the musical equivalent of working in a bank. Personally I've always preferred to be leaping about a stage in a rock'n'roll band, but I've also done plenty of acoustic shows because hey, a gig's a gig[109]. It's these shows that one must be particularly wary of, as you're swimming in dangerous waters. Some acoustic shows are fantastic, but there are those when you're not doing a gig as such, rather you're performing as a sort of flesh and blood stereo system – and just like an actual stereo system, nobody gives you a second glance or even acknowledges your existence. Sure, it sounded alright when that café said they'd pay $150 for an acoustic set, and as I feel compelled to accept pretty much any gig offered to me I naturally agree to do it, but by God it's depressing when you do. Generally you don't realise you've been hired as background music until a few songs into the set – initially you're hoping it's a cool bohemian café full of music fans – but then you get that sinking feeling of oh, it's one of *those* gigs. Finishing a song to be greeted by the gentle murmur of people continuing their conversations and ignoring you entirely is monumentally depressing, and even once you've worked out that it's nothing personal and these people are just not here for music, it's still an enormously deflating feeling to be playing your heart out when nobody cares. I've done plenty of these shows where people have spoken to me afterwards and said they'd really enjoyed it, and nice though that is you can't help but scream inwardly that you could have made that known *while* I was playing so I didn't feel quite so worthless all night. This seems to be much more of a thing in Australia than in England, and I think it's fair to say that England generally seems to value live music a little more than Australia does, and treats it with perhaps a little more respect. We were asked to do a show as an acoustic trio at a venue near Melbourne, as the musical entertainment at a poetry night. We performed two short sets during interludes of the poetry readings.

---

[109] Except when it's not.

We sat and watched a number of very talented poets, many of whom expressed to the crowd how nice it was to be able to perform like this and have people sit and listen and show them some respect and appreciation. And it was indeed very nice, except that when it came to our turn, we were entirely ignored by poets and audience alike, and shown neither respect nor appreciation, an apparently unwelcome intrusion into the higher intellectual pursuits that the evening was dedicated to. As is so often the case in this sort of scenario, you sit there wondering whether this is the nature of the beast or whether you're just really shit - and as you're a musician and thus existing in a world composed almost entirely of crippling self-doubt, the natural presumption to make is towards the latter.

You can't judge a gig by the amount of people, or lack of people, in attendance. I'm fairly (but not entirely) sure that I've never done a gig to nobody, but I'm also sure I've played to an audience of one on at least two occasions. I think the most I've played to would be about two thousand. There are many contributing factors to how enjoyable the gig is, and audience size isn't really one of them. I played an acoustic gig in a small Melbourne pub one cold winter's night, with my violin player Sally. After setting up we sat chatting by the window for an hour or so, with one eye keeping a watch on the people passing by to see who'd be coming into the pub. One guy arrived. And that was it. Nobody else. Well, nothing to do but to go for it, so we jumped on stage[110] and started playing. And everything went like a dream. The sound was utterly perfect[111] – vocals, guitar and violin wonderfully balanced to enable you to concentrate entirely on playing, instead of

---

[110] Left our seats by the window and walked three paces to the right and picked up our instruments.

[111] A rarer occurrence than an eclipse of the sun.

straining to hear your fellow musician and having to use a fair bit of guesswork as to what is going on, which is what happens at least half the time. And of course there was no background noise to contend with. As a result we played the songs as well as, if not better, than we ever had before. The dude at the bar *loved* it, which was just as well really as we had two sets to play. To this day it remains one of my favourite gigs.

A similarly sparsely attended event that was *not* one of my favourite gigs happened in Melbourne. We'd been booked to play a party for a motorbike club that my drummer was a member of. Also booked for the night was a troupe of "exotic dancers", the first and only time one of my bands has been the support act for strippers. We delayed and delayed starting our set in the hope of an audience arriving, but eventually resigned ourselves to the inevitable and did our thing to a crowd of four or five – half of whom were partners of people in my band. The best you can do is treat these sort of gigs as a free rehearsal. This was not the attitude of the dancers, who resolutely refused to do *their* thing for the entertainment of the bar staff and my band, to the eternal disappointment of my keyboard player. Turned out in the end that the party had been cancelled some weeks back, but nobody had informed us, the dancers, or the venue.

Talking of poor crowds and strippers reminds me of a short-lived venue in Melbourne's outer suburbs, one that we played at a couple of times. As I mentioned, it is not uncommon to find yourself door-watching at a gig, desperately hoping the next people to walk by will be coming in the venue to watch you, which to be honest is never a healthy pre-gig routine. But when your fee depends on door takings, you sometimes can't help yourself. The first time we played at this place, I was standing around outside for a while, watching a steady flow of punters walking into the club. I was somewhat surprised to see so many people, and with a spring in my stride I walked back into the venue anticipating a great show in a packed room. Only to find the place empty. This was rather confusing, until further investigation revealed that once inside the door you could go straight ahead into the band room, or you take a small dark staircase to the next floor. Turned out that on the next floor was a strip club. A very busy strip club. Doh.

One of the best audiences to play for is a bunch of young kids. This was something of a surprise to me to be honest. I never planned to become a children's entertainer, never saw myself as a potential Wiggle, but then we hatched a cunning scheme to improve our chances of getting booked for more festivals. Whenever you apply for a festival in Australia, they will ask if there is anything else you can offer[112], and will suggest ways in which you can help – some MC-ing perhaps (no chance), volunteering at the ticket office (yeah right), maybe a tutorial workshop (well, I can teach people how to roll the perfect joint but festival organisers seem to frown at this one), or some children's entertainment. Festivals are often family affairs, which means a lot of very bored young kids over the course of a weekend, and any chance to get someone else to entertain them for a bit will be snapped up by the parents. The way I saw it is that there would be a lot of young bands applying for these festivals, and

---

[112] Translation: we wish to wring every last possible drop of value from you if you're going to play here.

if they're anything like I was – or indeed any of my friends were – they would all be way too cool to even consider a children's concert. So if we offered a concert aimed at children, this would be a massive tick in our favour. And so it proved. The acceptance rate for the band leapt up when I did this, and as by this time I had kids myself, I'd already learnt a few of the staples – Old MacDonald Had A Farm, Incy Wincy Spider etc. So we worked out a whole acoustic set of traditional children's songs, jazzed them up a bit and put in some fancy little instrumental breaks to keep any parents in attendance entertained. This was a revelation, and these shows were always great fun. Unlike adults, kids have no fear of getting up and dancing and showing their appreciation. These performances were always fairly small, low-key morning affairs - until the last one we did, which was on a massive stage with an audience of several hundred. Backstage was milling with an assortment of children's entertainers, all of whom were real children's entertainers – they had the props, the outfits, and looked distinctly professional. We, well, we didn't. People were walking around dressed as zebras, monkeys, practicing their stilt-walking or balloon-animaling. Or both. We looked and felt about as out of place as, well, a rock'n'roll band amongst a bunch of professional children's entertainers. After an unsurprisingly flat show, where we found ourselves not so much slightly out of our depth as floundering around alone in the middle of the Atlantic Ocean, I decided that perhaps I'll be a bit more circumspect about offering this in future.

Festivals come in all shapes and sizes. There are the tiny little ones to which the description of festival seems to be pushing it somewhat, where someone has perhaps set up a small PA under a portable canvas gazebo in a pub garden. Location is all here. If there is food and beer readily available, fine weather, and perhaps a beach or a market, then you're onto a winner, but if not then they can be a decidedly depressing affair. Then you get the small town rural festivals where they utilise perhaps a couple of pubs and an RSL[113] in the town, which means they save a heap of cash on setting up a festival site but then have everything so spread out that any sense of community and/or festival is killed dead by the tyranny of distance. I've done a lot of these, and they're always a bit weird. For a start they need the entire town to be onboard with the whole festival concept, which they absolutely never are. So you get a bunch of enthusiastic festival goers out for a good time, mixed in with a bunch of miserable locals that are pissed off that a whole bunch of "people who aren't from around 'ere" are invading their town. These folks have no interest at all in perhaps enjoying a new experience, instead they focus on making sure they still do exactly the same thing as they always do on a Saturday night - which is usually getting drunk and losing money on the gaming machines, and perhaps having a fight. And woe betide anything or anyone that gets in their way. This applies to venue owners as well as punters. There will always be at least one pub landlord that has agreed to become part of the festival after months or pestering from the local festival committee on the basis that there's gold in them thar hills, but who really isn't into the whole idea, especially the whole idea of <spits> musicians. At one such happy gathering I was lucky enough to have my guitar stolen after the first show, although I didn't realise this until the next day when we got ready for an afternoon gig at the next pub on the list[114]. I only realised what had happened as we unloaded, which made things a little awkward. As I went off to the

---

[113] Returned Services League, an Australian variation on the Ex-Serviceman's Clubs in England. More on these later.

[114] Usually your band would be booked for a weekend, and all the acts end up playing 3-5 shows around the town, making sure that every band appearing gets to experience the really shit venue.

local cop shop to report the theft, the rest of the band were left to set up without me and do their best to entertain the audience, while I filled out forms and got generally pissed off and depressed about the whole thing. Unable to find another guitar I could borrow from a fellow musician, I returned to find that my band had upset the landlord by taking a drinks break after half an hour (we had a two-hour slot to fill) to reconvene and try and come up with a better plan of how to play a set with no singer/guitarist. As a result, said landlord had gone apeshit at the band, accusing them of ripping him off, an interesting tack to take given that he wasn't actually responsible for paying us. Despite my explaining what had happened, he was not in a forgiving mood and told me that in fact he was glad my guitar was stolen as it served me right for messing him around... which was another interesting take on the situation to be fair – being the victim of some form of pre-emptive karmic retribution by theft was one that I had not hitherto considered. In fact, he said, why don't you all just fuck off? Festival management arrived to calm things down, at which point he was slightly mollified and agreed that we could play a set after all (gee, thanks dude!) but only if I wasn't involved. This condition simply confused everybody, and we decided we would instead take the offer of just fucking off, if you don't mind. On a happier note, I got my guitar back a few days later, which was lucky, as if I hadn't then the Cathay Pacific baggage handlers would never have had the chance to smash it up six months later.

In another fine example of festival venues not being one hundred percent behind the concept that they've signed up for, we played a pub that was half full of festival punters and half full of regulars that were there to watch the cricket on TV. Rather than jumping feet-first into the festival spirit, the pub decided that they could cover all their bases by leaving the cricket on the telly while we played. This could possibly have worked – had the TV not been mounted on the wall *directly above the stage*. This led to a surreal show where we played a rocking set to a rather polarised audience, half of whom were dancing around the other half, who resolutely stood there watching the cricket. It was made no easier for me by the fact that I too really wanted to be watching the cricket[115], which was being broadcast only three feet above my head but entirely out of my line of vision.

I mentioned RSLs earlier – clubs for ex-armed forces types. I've done several shows in these slightly strange surroundings, populated almost entirely by sad old drunk geezers reminiscing over the good old days when they could travel abroad and shoot foreigners. Generally these also fall into the category of venues playing a part in a festival organised for the local community but doing so begrudgingly. They also have a problem with anyone wearing a hat – which makes things interesting when your whole band are committed hat-wearers. I've never quite understood the notion that wearing a hat is disrespectful to anyone, especially to people who actually wore a hat as part of their uniform. Also why it only applies to men – we were once told at one such establishment that our fiddle player could wear her hat, as she was a she, but the rest of us must remove ours. I've tried to get to the roots of this custom but, as far as I can tell, wearing a hat at the wrong time or place is rude simply because wearing a hat at the wrong time or place is rude. I can't find a better explanation than that. There appears to be no obvious origin. I was once thrown out of an RSL

---

115 After all, this was the 2010/11 Ashes series, with England in the midst of destroying Australia in some considerable style.

not because they objected to me openly rolling a spliff in the venue, but because I was wearing a hat at the time! They only let me back in when they realised I was part of the band and they had no choice.

We once attended a music awards ceremony at an RSL. Not really a "playing live" story, but here would seem as good a place as any to tell it. It was done as part of a festival, and as we were nominated for several awards we went along for a bit of a laugh - only to discover they were charging us $40 a head to get in. I've never been, but I'm pretty sure that's not how it works at the Oscars[116]. After initially being refused admittance into the main room for refusing to take our hats off[117], we relented and put our efforts into drinking all the free alcohol we could find, which as it turned out was a measly two bottles of really cheap wine for our table of six. Luckily, RSLs might not be keen on hats, but they do like cheap beer, so the alcohol mission was still accomplished relatively pain-free. The whole evening was a slightly bizarre pastiche of the sort of awards ceremonies you might see on the television, made all the weirder by the fact that none of the bands involved with the actual awards were performing – instead we got an assortment of speeches by RSL members and a couple of performances by musicians apparently unconnected to the whole event and/or festival. It must however be noted in the interests of unbiased reporting that in one of the great miscarriages of justice in all history, for all our nominations we won nothing, and as such carry nothing but bitter resentfulness towards everything connected with said event. Boo!

---

[116] I'm still disappointed that we didn't get one of those legendary Oscars gift bags, but with an RSL theme – perhaps a plastic bag with a crusty old beer coaster, a packet of old peanuts and a No Hats Here sticker.

[117] We fought hard for equal hat rights over the years.

One almighty pain in the arse with playing live is that if you're sick, there's bugger all you can do except suck it up and get on with it. And if you're doing a lot of shows on a regular basis, there is no avoiding the fact that at some point you will be ill. In fact, the more gigs you do the more likely you are to get ill, as a result of being on the road and at the mercy of exhaustion, poor diet, lack of sleep and excessive alcohol and/or drug consumption. Cancelling a show for sickness is considered seriously bad form, as the nature of the beast means that the cancellation will be the day before or – more likely - the day of the gig. This causes considerable inconvenience for the venue, and for yourself – especially if you've spent time, money and effort promoting the gig. So a sickness-induced cancellation should be kept safe. Hidden. Dark and deep in the vaults, not to be used unless at the uttermost end of need. I have resorted to it just once, when I had lost my voice. As a singer, losing your voice really gives you no choice, and I had to cancel on the morning of the gig. Not a big gig, just an acoustic show in a pub, so minimal disruption in the overall scheme of things. I'd previously done four or five enjoyable shows there, and I got on well with the owner and liked playing there. Nevertheless, said owner was furious with me for the cancellation - even though I whispered/croaked my bad news to her in person and was clearly incapable of playing – and she never gave me another gig or indeed spoke to me ever again. What can ya do?

Well, what you can and indeed must do is suffer and push on through. The show must go on and all that. It's not too hard to tough it out if you're a keyboard player[118], but it can be a hell of a tough night

---

118 You're probably sitting down already anyway and only using one hand half the time too, so you can even medicate on the go.

if you're the drummer. And I imagine horn players must struggle somewhat if they have a cold. But I don't think it's overly biased to suggest that it is toughest for the singer. Singing is physically draining at the best of times[119], and trying to do so with a head full of snot or a hacking cough is a bloody nightmare. Your breathing techniques are shot to bits and your range takes a sizeable cut at the top end. Many are the gigs I've done with a box of tissues sat on my guitar amp, which become a mountain of grossness piled up behind the amp by the end of the gig. I have a flask for such occasions too, filled with copious amounts of hot honey and lemon to help get me through the show. But here's the thing... you always get through it, and it's never as bad as you expect. And this is down to Doctor Stage. I don't know if the good Doctor is a man or a woman, I don't know if the Doctor has any form of corporeal existence, or whether he or she is pure spirit, a ghostly guardian angel of the boards we tread – but I do know that Doctor Stage is highly effective and always on call. Of course, there are killjoys out there that will assign all of the Doctor's miraculous healing abilities to simple adrenalin, but these are the sort of people who don't follow any social media accounts that post pictures of cute animals every day, because they're "grown adults", and as such they should be ignored at all times. Doctor Stage has treated me on any number of occasions with great efficacy, and although the price paid for the treatment post-show can be expensive, it's not nearly as costly as cancelling the show. On one memorable occasion I was rushed to hospital with breathing difficulties and an exceptionally painful sore throat, to be told I had chronic laryngitis and should rest up and try not to talk for a week. Unfortunately the next day was the final gig of a UK tour and I wasn't going to miss it for the world. Feeling like absolute crap I rocked up at the venue anyway, sat in silence for

---

119 Unless you're Lou Reed, in which case you could probably get away with not even waking up.

a couple of hours, my body aching and dreading what was to come, and then nervously took to the stage. At which point ~~the adrenalin kicked in~~ Doctor Stage enveloped me in a warm blanket of healing goodness and I sung as well as I've ever sung for the next hour or so. Thanks Doc!

Anyway, back to festivals. Once they break out of the town, things improve greatly. A dedicated festival site means things are being taken to a much more professional level, and all the nonsense incurred in playing local pubs disappears. Instead, you get dedicated stages and audiences who are there for the bands rather than the telly and the cheap parmigiana. I remember being rather taken aback the first time I played one. You see, there are many different types of audience to play to – your own fans for example, i.e. the folk that come along and actually pay to see your headline show at the pub or the club. There aren't many of them – that's why you're playing the pub – and if you get perhaps thirty or more then generally that's a pretty good result. Of course you'd probably get a lot more if you just did one show a year, but you need the gigs and the money, which is why you've played this town fifteen times already this year even though it's not yet August. Then there are the times you play to someone else's fans, as the result of a support slot. On the one hand a great chance to play to people who haven't seen you before. On the other hand, a great chance to be entirely ignored by the handful of people who have bothered to turn up early enough to see your set. Then are those places full of people who don't really like music and treat the band as a real inconvenience, or the venues where you are simply background music and just ignored. But the crowds at a decent festival are generally brilliant. For a start, they've all come along, probably for the whole weekend, to watch bands. Bands they know and love, and bands they've never heard of. Either way, they've spent a lot of money on a ticket and they're going to bloody well enjoy themselves. It's a wonderful feeling to come and play on a big stage with a cracking lighting rig, top-notch sound systems operated by <gasp> real sound personnel, and all in front of a thousand receptive people who are all out to enjoy themselves. These folk spend money too, and you can really shift some merchandise at a decent festival. Well, you can with an afternoon show. This is when people spend that money on bands. After a certain point – somewhere around 7pm according to my observations – they continue to spend money, only this time it all goes to the bar. Which is a shame, but on the plus side they're now getting drunk which means the dancefloor goes off, which is a fair trade I reckon. As a result of all this, you get to spend a weekend feeling like a proper rock star. Well, until you go back to your tent anyway.

Talking of tents, the biggest festival appearance of my career was very nearly scuppered entirely by a tent[120]. Now up until this point I'd had a pretty good relationship with tents, or at least with my cosy little 1-man dome that had served me well for many years, but on this occasion I had my family with me and was debuting our brand new fancy 6-berth tent. We had a lunchtime show on the main stage of one of Australia's biggest festivals. We'd played a late show the night before on a smaller stage, resulting in a mildly hedonistic evening, tempered slightly by the knowledge of the big show to come the next day. Feeling slightly the worse for wear the next morning I

---

120 Although if it could talk I suspect the tent might place the blame squarely at my feet. You can make up your own mind in a couple more sentences time.

nevertheless began to prepare, freshening up with a dip in the pool[121] before heading back to the tent to get ready. With time in hand, the opportunity presented itself to get the awning of my tent functioning correctly, to enable a little sun/rain protection while sitting outside to restring my guitar. Family size tents with proper metal poles were a little beyond my range of previous experience, and unfortunately I tried just a little bit too hard to connect the necessary poles together. My hand slipped, resulting in my thumb being jammed between the poles and me screaming "fuuuuuuuuuuccckkkk" at the top of my voice across the campsite. As I extracted the wounded digit from the camping apparatus, the blood began pouring out and the realisation dawned that I kind of needed that thumb for playing guitar. Half an hour of wandering around searching for a first aid station proved fruitless, and it became clear that I was going to have to be my own medic. Which of course means one thing and one thing only – gaffer tape. With my wound washed and dressed and a double helping of painkillers consumed, I was feeling a little better and made my way to the stage to start setting up for our early afternoon show. As I warmed up backstage it became abundantly clear that playing guitar today was going to be a) quite tricky and b) bloody painful. I was also beginning to feel somewhat nauseous and more than a little shaky, which I attributed to the injury rather than the fact that I hadn't eaten since the previous afternoon and had forgotten all about breakfast as a result of my accident. But I figured Doctor Stage would turn up soon enough and see me through. Sure enough, as we took the stage to one of the biggest crowds I have ever played to, perhaps the peak of my career thus far, the first twenty minutes of the hour-long set went by relatively smoothly as I successfully adjusted my guitar playing style on the fly in an attempt to hold on to the plectrum. Then my

---

[121] Yep, we had an artist-only swimming pool on site. Not an everyday occurrence, this.

body started to send a number of worrying red flag alerts to my brain – firstly it informed me that I really should have had some form of fuel prior to the gig, as in fact the last sustenance I had provided it was four pints of beer the night before. Secondly, it informed me that while it was dedicating 100% of its runtime to keeping me upright and able to sing, it was as a result powerless to dedicate any further resources to combating the increasingly urgent need to vomit. In a rare instance of dereliction of duty, Doctor Stage had – perhaps understandably – decided to finish early that day, and leave me to it. I spent a couple of songs nervously looking around the stage for a dark corner in which I could maybe throw up without anybody noticing, but I didn't fancy my chances. Such dark corners have been a feature of 90% of shows I've ever done, but it was just my luck that that day, for once in my musical career, I was actually playing on a stage with a fantastic lighting rig in front of a bloody big crowd and no dark corners whatsoever. With my condition failing to improve as the set continued, I realised drastic action was required, and during an instrumental break in one number I casually sauntered over towards the bass amp. Hoping that the audience attention was on the fiddle player as she soloed away, I bent down behind the bass amp and – still playing guitar – finally chundered, barfing up nothing but liquid, but heroically directing it away from both myself and the bass amp. Feeling a little better, I looked up to see a number of people staring at me, with a look that suggested they were now firmly regretting their choice of seating. But a quick swig of water and I was back to the mic to finish the song. I made it through the rest of the set, but it was some considerable distance from being the best performance I've given, and I knew I'd royally screwed up one of the best opportunities the band had ever had.

Sometimes a night is simply cursed, and absolutely nothing you can do will make it better, or indeed remove the searing burn of it from your memory for the rest of your life. One such occasion was a show we played in Fulham, in the south west of London. We were pretty excited about the night as we jumped into the van and began the journey into the capital. We had a full coachload of people making the journey to see us, and the night was being filmed for live broadcast on some cable tv channel. Woo-hoo! As we joined the M25[122], the singer Robbie called the booker to double-check what time we were playing. Only for the booker to tell us that we weren't on the bill at all. What the fuck? Dude, we're halfway there and we've got a coach load of fans coming down! *Well you're not playing, sorry, there must have been a mix up.* Man, you can't do this to us! *Well... if you come down we might be able to fit you in at the end of the night, but it will mean going on stage at 1am.* Oh come on dude, we've got a bloody coach organised, we can't do that! *Sorry guys, that's just the way it is.* OK, listen, we need this gig to happen or we're letting down a lot of people, what's it going to take to get us playing before 11pm? In the end, what it took was a gram of cocaine, the offer of which made the booker only too happy to screw over another unfortunate band instead of us. But that was just the beginning of the problems. After we'd loaded in we had some time to kill, so we went and sat in a café across the road from the venue. As we all sat there, despondently gazing out the window with most of the earlier excitement drained away by the uncertainty of how things were now going to pan out, we watched a car plough straight into an old guy crossing the road, throwing the poor chap up in the air before he landed with a sickening thud right outside the window. The emergency services were on the scene in no time, but this fellow had been killed instantly. This put

---

122 For those of you who don't know, the M25 is an enormous car-park that encircles London, used as a motorway at night.

paid to any remaining excitement we had for the night, and everyone was badly shaken up as we made our way back into the venue. Only to find that someone[123] had stolen the drummer's bag, complete with all his sticks, brushes, spare parts and drum stool. We desperately tried to rustle up replacement drum parts, but the band on before us didn't have a drummer and the band on after us had yet to arrive. We attempted to get assistance from the booker, who was now so coked up that he didn't give a flying fuck about it, and in the end the drummer was reduced to sitting on a plastic chair instead of his drum stool, using the only drum sticks available - two crappy old sticks well past their best that we found in a cupboard backstage. Well it could be worse, we could have no sticks at all. Oh wait, it is worse. Where the hell are our coach load of fans? The coach, it turned out, had got lost on route. On we went and, after a few lacklustre songs with some very uncertain drumming, fate – clearly not happy with the miserable hand she'd dealt us thus far – decreed that Robbie's acoustic guitar was about due to break down. Luckily this happened in a song that had a section in the middle where everybody stops playing except the acoustic guitar. Just as our coach turns up and our loyal fans walk in, we get to this part of the song, and everybody stops. And there's no acoustic guitar. So we all stand there looking at each other waiting for someone to rescue the situation, but nobody is switched on enough to cover for the acoustic, so the song just... stopped. Instead of getting the acoustic break, what we actually got was the drummer shouting "fuck this, I've had enough of this shit" and walking off. The rest of us just stood there – lest you forget, this show was being broadcast live on cable tv – looking like idiots, overwhelmed by all the events of the night thus far and totally incapable of rescuing the situation. Luckily our drummer sheepishly returned to his chair and we held it

---

123 Probably someone from the unfortunate other band that had been cancelled due to their inability to bribe the booker with sufficient cocaine.

together long enough to complete a couple more songs – badly, but completed nonetheless – and that was the end of that. Well, nearly. There was still time for Robbie to get in a fight with the booker who was demanding more cocaine before we left, but thankfully the only remaining bad luck for the evening was confined to our roadie Den, who was eating a bag of chips and accidentally ate one of those little paper packets of salt - which he mistook for a chip in the darkness of the van. Which at least cheered the rest of us up quite considerably.

Something that has caused me much distress over the years has been the setlist – that is, the list of songs that a band has onstage so they all know which songs are coming next. Going to gigs as a teenager it was seen as a very worthy pursuit to liberate a band's setlist as a memento after they leave the stage. If you were lucky you could perhaps get one signed! The setlist comes in three varieties[124]:

1. Neatly typed up in a bold sans-serif font (A4, capitalisation optional)

These people are far too organised, printing out setlists as needed. This valuable stress-saving setlist is a winner with one major drawback – the numerous wonky arrows, scribbles and in-retrospect-I-could-have-made-this-clearer-style shorthand alterations you must make if you want to change the song order around.

---

[124] I have to be honest, my experience only goes a certain distance here... When it comes to arena tours with their massive stage productions, does the humble setlist get pushed aside? For all I know there's a little setlist monkey backstage with an earpiece link up to all the musicians by which the monkey can communicate the next song.

2. Neatly hand-written with thick black marker pen (A4, capitalisation essential)

A.k.a. The Classic. Written most often in the space between the soundcheck and the performance, allowing for maximum flexibility in choice of songs. Neatly written it is a thing of beauty, art in itself. Drawbacks include the need for carrying some plain A4 paper and decent marker pens at all times[125]. Also many musicians have handwriting that could make a doctor blush, and it's important that these musicians don't get the job even if they want it.

3. Scrawled in biro on the back of a cigarette packet (Size: the smaller the better)

It doesn't have to be a cigarette packet. It could equally be a shopping receipt, a large rizla, or a hand. Usually two different colours of ink from when the first pen runs out. Second colour will be written much more hurriedly. Honestly, what are you people thinking? Sort yourselves out.

I flirted with number one for a little while, but soon returned to my roots, the classic number two. We've all resorted to number three before at some point, it's unavoidable, but there are people that actually make a habit of it. A preference for it even. This is not acceptable behaviour.

I like being able to choose the songs I think will work best after judging the venue, how I feel at the time, and the general vibe of the night. In the early days this was dead easy. We simply played all our

---

125 Regular setlist writers will have at least three dried up marker pens in their bag.

songs, and hoped they lasted as long as our allotted time on stage. After a while you get to make changes here and there as you write more material. If you stick around long enough you find yourself with a back catalogue of a hundred songs to choose from. Which sounds like a lot, but we can perhaps reduce the figure a little. If you've been around for a decade then you'll have likely had numerous personnel changes, and some of the band may have only joined relatively recently. They have never played more than a handful of songs from your earlier years, so we can probably half the original hundred as a minimum. Out of the remaining fifty, there will be songs that you are sick to death of now and simply don't want to play. Let's drop another ten. From the remaining forty, there's fifteen that don't really work that well in the live environment. Twenty-five is what's left to work with, which is a long way from the hundred you had on paper. This is still a great choice to have a for a forty-five-minute gig. It's more than enough to work with for a headline slot, with some options for changing it around. It's not enough for those awful gigs you stumble upon from time-to-time that work on the format of three sets of forty-five minutes each, but that's another story. From your twenty-five songs, you'll have the bare bones of a set in your head anyway – perhaps a really good pair of opening numbers, or a great four-song combination that you always finish with – and from there you add the other tracks as required. The setlist writer develops a knowledge of exactly how long each songs takes and knows the key of each one, as well as which ones not to put next to each other. It's a tricky thing to get right, and you never know you've got it wrong until it's too late. For the successful band it's more about balancing the songs they want to play with what the audience want to hear, which will rarely match. For us lesser mortals, it's about having a set built to impress the first-time listener. Built with a plan B in mind, so that if you suddenly find that the crowd really do like you and they all start dancing, you can keep them dancing, rather than sticking to your guns and watching everyone go and sit down during the epic atmospheric slower track. Once they sit down, it's much harder to get them back up again. I'd usually rush off a few setlists for the band, and then write my own with all its assorted notations – prompts for remembering lyrics on new songs, reminders for when I need a capo[126] and for which fret said capo must rest on. Occasionally perhaps some boobs and cocks that someone has drawn on when I wasn't looking. Numerous times I'd find myself stressing out minutes before going on as I desperately tried to get the right setlist down on paper, knowing I still needed five minutes after this to find the gaffer tape and stick them down on the stage.

I briefly mentioned sound checking previously. This is a mundane task which may well be done by an inhouse sound dude/dudette, or perhaps you've paid for your own, or perhaps you're in a venue where you must – uh-oh – do your own. There are venues where the PA is already well set up well for the room and it's only mildly stressful to find a halfway decent sound. Then there are the venues where you get shown to a dark cupboard out the back, filled up with all manner of crap, amongst which given enough time and perhaps some light you may be lucky enough to find the various parts of the pubs PA

---

[126] Launching straight into a song without your capo when that song should be played with a capo on the sixth fret is easily done. Usually you realise straight away that something doesn't sound quite right but you don't have the time to dwell on it, then the band come in and start looking confused and you finally realise what you've done when you notice the keyboard player gesturing wildly at the capo that's sitting at rest on the guitar's headstock instead of doing its job on the sixth fret.

system, which will be woeful[127] and *will not*, I repeat *will not*, have any monitors.

Once you've finally assembled a PA into working[128] order from the parts of several PAs that are definitely not in working order, you have to start playing to get some idea of sound levels. But when you want to adjust those levels, you have to stop playing and get offstage[129]. For the singer/guitarist, this means unplugging your guitar each time you need to walk off and adjust the sound, before then plugging back in to see what it sounds like. Repeat until finished. Why not get one of the other band members to do this I hear you cry? Well, the drummer needs to be playing as he's not miked up, except perhaps his kick drum, so we all have to work around his levels with our amps. You can't ask the bass player for obvious reasons, and if you ask the guitarist – any guitarist – you will get a mix that all guitarists are experts at, the defining feature of which is of course really really loud guitar. This is much easier at smaller gigs when the desk to operate the PA is crammed in the corner of the stage itself to save space elsewhere, and you find yourself making adjustments by simply leaning over the bass player and reaching over his amp to try and find the faders and nudge them up or down without falling over and breaking your guitar. Much as I loathe all the fucking around that these scenarios

---

[127] Nobody just throws a decent PA system into a dark cupboard full of crap, a decent one is looked after and probably left set up to show it off.

[128] To a certain value of the word working. Mind you, after decades of this crap, I reckon you could show me to any dark cupboard full of odd bits of busted PA gear in any venue in the world and I could put something together that works. I'm like the A-Team, but for PAs instead of armoured vehicles.

[129] The term offstage carries a broad meaning, and can mean "getting offstage by walking over to the side of the stage and going down a staircase before exiting via a door into the backstage area" as well as "getting offstage by stepping over the microphone lead that's gaffer-taped to the dirty threadbare paisley carpet and, well, now you're at the bar".

involve, the positive is that at least the sound is done by someone who cares and knows what they're after, rather than the surly inhouse sound engineer who is already half-pissed and who disappears for a smoke every two minutes, and forgets to turn the vocal mics on until the third song.

Before any gig, there's a period of waiting ranging from bloody hours to literally seconds between arriving and performing, and once you've written the setlists there are plenty of other things that can take up your time and keep your mind from dwelling on the coming performance. Actually I was very rarely worried about the performance itself, my main concern would usually be worrying if anybody was going to turn up. A long wait is torturous, and I've spent an awfully large part of my life hanging around and killing time before a gig, in a state of not-quite-able-to-relax. A short wait can be tricky too as you don't get much time to get into the right headspace. No wait at all is just horrible. Thanks to some overly ambitious scheduling from yours truly, we were playing in Adelaide on a Saturday night, followed by a Sunday show at 5pm near Melbourne. We figured if we left by 8am we should be able to cover the 700-kilometre journey with a bit to spare. Luckily there had been enormous storms that weekend and the rivers were overflowing, and as they came south to the coast – and across our route – the flooding began in earnest. The subsequent road closures made for a bewildering journey as we tried every which way possible to make it through the water[130] and ended up hurtling around the countryside and covering about 150 kilometres on top of what we should have done, getting progressively more nervous about the increasing possibility that we'd not be able to

---

130 Short of actually going through the water.

make the gig. We called the venue and promised we'd be there, which was bravely optimistic, nevertheless we made it dead on 5pm. We unloaded straight to the stage, the other band having just finished as we got there, and away we went. I didn't even have time for a piss and spent the second half of the gig wondering if you could die from your bladder exploding.

I've had the pleasure of playing at quite a few weddings over the years. I've never tried to get these gigs, and I've always been slightly surprised when anyone asks if I'll play at theirs. Um, wait, what... you want *my* band? For your *wedding*? With our predominantly original material that none of your guests will have ever heard before? Are you *sure* that's what you want? Sorry, you'll pay me how much? Count us in! I gave up offering to learn a song especially for a wedding very early on, when I once agreed to play a song I really did not like and found that it used an alternative tuning that I'd never used before[131], so not only did I have to learn a new song I had to learn a whole new set of chords too. I was asked to play the song with my fiddle player as the bride made the long walk from the car park to the top of a picturesque but exceptionally windy[132] cliff overlooking the Bass Strait. This sort of performance ranks very high on the list of those that you *really* don't want to fuck up, and I was finding this song a very easy song to fuck up. I scraped through unwounded in the end, despite screwing up some of the words and having to make up a couple of lines of my own on the fly. Terrified that they'd be mad at me, I tried and failed to avoid the happy couple after the ceremony, but luckily it turned out nobody had noticed anyway – it was the

---

131   That's basically any of them.
132   And man, whoever designed the acoustics on that cliff top didn't have a clue.

bride's choice of song and she'd been so wrapped up in the wedding that she didn't even remember us playing. Nevertheless I vowed that was the end of special wedding requests.

I've played in some odd places. Quite a few odd places in fact. I once had the pleasure of playing a show in a non-alcoholic pub. I know, I know. Look... this was far less of a strange thing at the time than it seems to me now, but perhaps my many years of living in Australia have over-emphasised how stupid the idea seems to me when I think about it today. I mean a non-alcoholic pub, *really*? Perhaps this sort of thing could have worked in London in the early nineties, but not in Craptown in the home counties. I'm not someone who feels it is essential to drink beer to have a good night out, but I do like the option to be available if I've gone to a pub. A non-alcoholic pub is basically a late-night café with no food or hot drinks but hey look the soft drinks fridge is still working and it dispenses free glasses. Although thinking about it, you would have been perfectly welcome to smoke, so there was that I suppose. I recall the gig being an unsurprisingly politely received show, that was okay in a moderately bland sort of way that neither offended nor enamoured, in equal measure. We passed up the opportunity of more free Fanta afterwards and sped off as fast as we could to the nearest actual alcoholic pub. Which is of course *all* of the other pubs. I think it lasted a few months, a bravely optimistic[133] attempt to find enough English people to go out at night and socialise with other English people, and that were happy to do so on the proviso that there will be absolutely no alcohol involved whatsoever.

---

[133] Some may say wildly optimistic.

We did a gig on a ship once. Nothing too odd about that, I mean every cruise ship has bands onboard right? Well yes, but this wasn't a cruise ship, this was a genuine old sailing ship from the 1800s, a twin-mast schooner that was a thing of real beauty. But perhaps lacking the facilities of your average cruise ship. The five of us arranged ourselves and our acoustic instruments in a row along the port-side of the ship, between the foremast and the mainmast, ever wary of the boom on the gaff sail[134] and its potential capacity to send us all flying overboard in one mighty swing. As we sailed out into the bay we began to play, and I realised that playing guitar and singing while standing on a "stage" that rocked and rolled with the motion of the waves was no easy task. After briefly considering the option of gaffer-taping my feet to the deck, I instead opted to lean back against the handrail around the deck for support. This was a risky choice, as the rail came about halfway up my thigh – so I could lean for additional support, but if I relied on it completely I could be man overboard before you could say shiver me timbers. This was one of only a handful of gigs I've done where I felt genuine fear and considered the possibility that my life could actually be in danger, which can rather knock you out of your stride. Halfway through the set the heavens opened and we finished the set down in the hold, which doubled as sleeping quarters and the galley. Oh the fun of trying to get a double bass down the hatch and the ladder and into the hold! But, nevertheless, an all-time favourite gig.

Continuing the theme of playing gigs on transportation, we once did a show on the back of a vintage VW camper van, converted into

---

134 My knowledge of sailing terminology far outstrips my knowledge of musical terminology.

a small flatbed truck, in which form it was used as a mobile coffee shop, complete with enormous sun umbrella. Still, at least it looked quite classy, a step above the gigs on the back of huge commercial trucks that have been driven into country festivals as a cheap staging option. *Yeah, drive the truck into that field mate and just pull back the awning on one side, that'll look great! Ya want me to give it a clean, I just transported two hundred tons of grime and dirt across the continent? Nah mate, she'll be 'right, musicians don't mind a bit of dirt.* Well we sort of do mind actually. It's one thing being in your standard grubby old venue - most of which have a stage in a room that hasn't seen daylight since the builders put the ceiling in and which exist in a permanently dull just-about-light which makes cleaning a little tough at the best of times – but it's another thing entirely to be sliding around in grease in broad daylight on a flatbed truck, wrecking your trousers when you foolishly go down on your knees to open up your guitar case and then writing off your nice new shirt when you finish and start winding up cables, all of which attract dirt like a magnet[135] thanks to being covered in years of gaffer tape residue. We did one festival show on the back of a massive – and of course filthy - Powercor[136] truck, covered in a mass of assorted Powercor advertising for good measure, and it was a hugely satisfying and deliciously ironic moment when we blew the power out halfway through our set. We finished off acoustically, sitting in front of the truck on the nice clean grass, which was rather lovely.

Another venue that sticks in my mind was outside of a brewery at a regional festival in Victoria. Now I'm all on board with the notion of a

---

135 I am aware that dirt is not generally magnetic.
136 An Australian electricity provider.

gig at a brewery, no problem there. A good chance of some decent, free beer for a start. We were shown to the "stage", which as we've already established is a word with a wide range of possible definitions. In this case it was a patch of gravel in a courtyard outside the building. Those of you lucky enough to have performed with a band on gravel will of course be aware of just what a wonderful surface gravel is to set up a band on. Drums are especially suited to an uneven floor that has a tendency to move, in fact I'm pretty sure the first drum kit ever designed was done so with the express intention that it be used only on a patch of gravel[137]. But the drummer's tribulations that day paled in comparison to my own. I find it impossible to perform without a constant shuffling to and fro of the feet as I sing and play guitar, and what happens when you do this on gravel is that you become a sort of human gravel-drill, suitable possibly for some form of low-grade exploratory mining, perhaps for long-lost gold coins. Luckily the gravel in this instance appeared to be piled up so thick that there was no danger of me reaching the bottom. After a few songs I was standing in a hole about a foot deep and having to adopt the Lemmy from Motorhead microphone technique. Eventually I gave up trying to fill the hole and found it easier just to keep adjusting the microphone stand after every song as I sank further and further into the Earth's crust.

Just as gravel is renowned as the ideal flooring for a stage, glass is of course known for its wonderful acoustic properties. We rocked up to a venue once to find some wag had extended their room to incorporate a stage in what amounted to a glass conservatory. As the

---

[137] This is of course why the drum rooms in all quality recording studios are carpeted with gravel.

horrors of what awaited us rapidly dawned, I quickly realised I was in for another of those nights when you really wish you'd stuck at that car-washing job – I mean by now I could be in charge of the staff that actually clean the cars. I could be handing out buckets and chamois leathers, instead of getting deafened by the noise of three amplifiers and a drumkit being reflected off three huge glass panels straight into my ears. There is no way on Earth you can sound good in a room like this, and you are absolutely powerless to do anything about it other than suck it up and make sure you never come back. The audience however just presume that the band sounds shit because the band is shit, having little or no concept of the notion that perhaps the band are having an even worse time of it than they are. All in all this gig was about as much fun as a week camping at the end of a busy airport runway.

Which isn't to say that all unusual venues are rubbish, although usually the acoustics will be. This is particularly true of anywhere open to the elements of nature, but as long as the wind isn't too bad then it can be rather delightful. I've never managed to play a gig on a beach in England[138], but it's happened a few times in Australia. There is definitely something to be said for having a stage set up on the beach[139], facing the ocean across a stretch of glorious sand and palm trees, and playing your set as the sun goes down. Actually I'd be pretty happy if all venues incorporated some form of sea element. We did a festival which included a couple of shows in a surf club, a very ordinary venue in general, but one that scored big by having us set up so as we looked over the sea as we played. Once we'd finished, instead

---

138 Phew!
139 A proper stage, not just some speakers on the sand, or a pile of specially imported gravel.

of sitting at the bar in clothes dripping with sweat, we stepped down onto the beach and into the wonderfully cool ocean. There is no more perfect way to relax and cool off from a show than a refreshing dip in the sea, and I considered that in future perhaps I should write some sort of ocean swim clause into gig contracts. Sadly this proved impractical. The nearest I got to repeating the experience was a show at a festival that had a Pool Party Stage. Nice as a post-performance dip in the pool was, it doesn't really compare to the Great Southern Ocean. Still, beggars can't be choosers.

Something that has become more popular in recent years has been the humble house concert. On the face of it these are a recipe for absolute disaster, but I've done a few of them that have been fantastic gigs. The hosts have usually been generous, courteous and anxious to do anything they can to make you comfortable. Sure, power outlets can be an issue, but copious amounts of free food and drink more than make up for this, and the percentage of drunken twats is normally much lower than the average pub gig. The more laid-back nature of these gigs seems to make for a much better connection with the audience. I did one in Tasmania where it was more of an informal chat in a beautiful garden, interspersed with the odd song, and it was all very lovely. Naturally they're not immune from being crap though – we once did a house concert in Melbourne and there were about fifty or so people in attendance when we turned up. This should be great thought I, but I had failed to account for the fact that it was a lovely night and everyone was out in the back garden. We set up in the lounge room as directed, and proceeded to play two one-hour sets, during which time three people came and watched us and the rest continued drinking in the back garden, to all intents and purposes oblivious to our presence. As we packed up and got ready to leave, monumentally disappointed with the whole thing, our drunken host approached us and said they were all ready to come inside and watch us. And then got very angry when we said actually we've finished and we're leaving now. He then told us we could get fucked if we thought we were getting paid, at which point I reminded him that he'd actually paid us on arrival. Ha!

12.
ON THE ROAD

THE ROADIE

The roadie is at best an honourable, age-old profession. The finest roadies in the world know everything that could go wrong and are prepared for absolutely anything as a result. They can restring a guitar in the dark in the time it takes a Formula One pit-crew to change a set of tyres, and then hand the guitar back perfectly in tune. They can fix *anything* and have a tool for *everything*.

As you may have guessed, the best roadies tend not to work at the lower end of the band ladder. Down at the lower end you get the worst roadies, who simply tend not to work at all. They range from mates you've managed to convince to come long and lift stuff, so that you don't have to, to more naïve mates who've actually volunteered to come along and lift stuff, so that you don't have to. Neither are likely to last very long. Either:

1. They will refuse to do it again because sod that mate, my back's killing me after travelling home from the gig in the back of the van on top of the speaker cabinets and when you went around that roundabout too fast they all collapsed and I spent the next five miles trying to get out from under the drums and I didn't get

paid a bloody penny, or

2. You will refuse to let them do it again because last time they got absolutely rat-arsed and dropped two grand's worth of guitar amp down a flight of stairs before passing out and pissing themselves in the van on the way home.

In fact, no roadie is considerably better than a shit roadie, and you're better off asking a complete stranger to help lift the bass amp than one of your pissed mates.

But while I've never experienced the joy of touring with a bona-fide proper roadcrew to back me up, I've experienced on many occasions the joy of touring with someone who aspired to be just like a professional roadie. We have met Den several times already, and after being fired from a couple of my bands as a bass player, he reinvented himself as a roadie. I think this was partly due to a need to be involved – we were at one point sharing a house and were best mates, so by being a roadie he was still able to be involved after leaving the band, which suited us both. Also we had roadied together for another band a couple of times, under the tutelage of an actually rather good roadie whose name I feel terribly guilty about not remembering, as he was a lovely chap who sadly died at far too young an age. We witnessed first-hand how to roadie correctly – the roadie must have his own equipment to do his job properly, the main essentials being a torch, gaffer tape, pliers and at least a couple of screwdrivers. But a good roadie will also have a bag of supplies full of such necessities as spare guitar strings, spare cables, a soldering iron, batteries and such like. Den saw how to do the job and thought yeah, I've got my own bum-bag, I can do that.

And Den did indeed have a wide range of roadie skills, presumably bestowed magically upon him by The Gods following a meeting at The Crossroads. These skills included the ability to:

- detune a guitar
- scrounge cigarettes from the band
- lose the gaffer tape
- restring a guitar with the wrong strings
- scrounge food from the band
- injure himself in every way imaginable[140]
- disappear when the band is ready to leave
- scrounge beer from the band
- make everyone in the band feel slightly better about themselves by way of comparison

In fairness, much of the above could and indeed does apply to many roadies, but he did seem to be abundantly blessed in this department. There were many, many times that Den royally fucked up, but I feel I should balance this by coming to his defence a little – our stage was always meticulously tidy, as Den was a master of taping down leads so that we wouldn't fall over them. So much so that at times you'd find yourself bumping into something mid-song, and find it was Den creeping around behind you with more gaffer tape for an errant stage cable. I'm sure that had I stopped moving about for more

---

140 Bloody hell dude, how did you break your foot? Oh I saw something that looked like a football, so I ran up and kicked it. But it was actually a lump of cement.

than a couple of minutes then I would have found my feet gaffer-taped to the stage. He would willingly lift all the gear into and out of the venue, and was always, always a good laugh (indeed, even in a bad mood he was still someone to have a good laugh *at*). I'd venture as far as to say that Den would have been a genuine asset if he hadn't such a propensity for making massive fuck ups. After one gig, most of the band was going back to the singer Robbie's house for a bit of a party, and they'd gone on ahead. I was still at the venue, along with my girlfriend and all my gear – Den was going to drive us back in his car. To his credit, he got all the gear loaded up in the car, even going so far as to remember my girlfriend's bag, which had all our essentials in it, like money, keys, cigarettes and hash. At this point, I'm sure you'll agree, Den has done his job to the letter. And then he was gone. Half an hour later, my girlfriend and I are still at the venue, the bar is closed, and we can't find Den anywhere. As we have no bag thus no money we are unable to even use the payphone to call anyone, let alone get a cab home, and at 1am there's a very limited number of people you can contact anyway. On top of which, we're not quite in pre-mobile phone days here, but only a few people had them. Luckily, one of those people was the soundman, still there packing up his van. I called Robbie at his house to tell him Den had gone missing. What do you mean gone missing, he's here mate! Well can you ask him if he realises he's maybe fucking forgotten something, like me and my missus? <muffled voices, swearing>.

As luck would have it, the soundman was going in the direction of Robbie's house, so we ended up getting a lift. But by the time we got there, Den had gone. Knowing that he had all my gear in the car, he thought he'd better get it all back to my place, so he set off from Robbie's. But disaster struck as the car broke down on the way, and Den decided to leave the car and walk home. I still have palpitations now when I think of my Telecaster, Fender Twin and large custom pedal board sitting in the back of Den's car all night in the middle of nowhere. Well, when I say the middle of nowhere, that's not strictly true. Den phoned me in the morning and told me I better find a way to get my gear, as it had sat in his broken-down car all night. What do you bloody mean it's sat in your car, where?! With no small degree of urgency I went to find the car, which was about five hundred yards away from Robbie's house - meaning that Den had driven five hundred yards from Robbie's, broken down, and then decided that rather than walking back to Robbie's, the sensible course of action would be to walk ten miles home in the other direction. Still, nothing was lost other than a little bit more faith in Den, and to be fair there had never been much of that in the first place.

Most of the time I would simply not have a roadie. A spare guitar in case of malfunction or string breakage, sitting there tuned up and ready to go, is the ideal scenario, but oft times there wouldn't be room in the vehicle/s to take a spare on the road. And I tended to break a fair number of guitar strings, a result of playing them too hard and a tendency to sweat a lot on stage, which catastrophically weakens the strings. So I'd have to meticulously prepare before every gig, making sure a plentiful and clearly labelled supply of spare guitar strings were ready to go at the side of the stage, along with the requisite tools to change them. If a string broke, I could change it within two minutes and the band were good enough to carry on without me if this situation arose, but this is hardly ideal. In the end, to prevent this situation occurring I would put new strings on before each performance. This is an expensive solution, but still preferable to using most of the roadies I've experienced. One chap, Max I think his name was, was no technician, but was good enough for lifting stuff and doing his share of driving. That is so long as you're happy to be absolutely fucking terrified while in the van, which Max drove at breakneck speed while aiming for every bird foolish enough to be on the road ahead of us, as if he was on some form of roadkill-related bonus pay. After narrowly avoiding a head on collision with a massive truck as he attempted to end the life of an unsuspecting pigeon, Max was banned from driving forthwith. He never came on tour with us again.

THE VAN

The tour bus is, in popular culture, a luxury vehicle full of copious supplies of drugs, alcohol and groupies, a comfortable home away from home wherein the hard-working musician can enjoy some well-deserved rest and relaxation on route to the next show. Band vans, however, are beaten-up unreliable beasts held together by gaffer tape, often with only a couple of actual seats, and liable to cost in repairs the equivalent of recording three new studio albums every year.

I was nineteen when I got my first band van. I was playing solely as a duo, me on acoustic guitar and Den on bass, thus we had absolutely no need for a van whatsoever. So naturally when we ran into someone who was selling an old Ford Transit for fifty quid, we jumped at the chance. Sure, it was a piece of shit, but we had time on our hands as well as a Haynes manual[141], and there was surely no problem that our

---

141 Basically an instruction manual showing how everything works and fits together in your vehicle – hugely useful in theory, but in practice only useful if the user is mechanically competent (e.g. not us).

youthful enthusiasm could not conquer. My parents were on holiday, so we could park the van on their driveway and work on it there. Hell, it would probably be ready to go by the time they returned anyway. We handed over our fifty quid and set off on the journey home, about six miles. This took just under three hours, making for an average speed of a dizzying two miles per hour. It would work when the battery was connected, but the connectors *for* the battery didn't match the connectors *on* the battery. With no gaffer tape to hand, the only way to get it to work was to balance the connectors on the battery terminals and drive. When the momentum of driving meant that the connectors had slid off the terminals, we had to stop and re-sit the connectors. This happened approximately every ten yards. Still, we made it home in the end and set right to work. With the engine looking buggered and in need of being stripped down pretty much entirely, we prioritised the most pressing matter and spray painted the band name onto the side. An hour or two later it was clear that we'd bitten off more than we could chew, and the van remained destined not to fulfil its, er, destiny. It did however remain exactly where it was, to the absolute delight of my parents when they returned home from holiday. A week or two later we got it towed away for scrap, which I think cost another fifty quid.

Mindful of this, a couple of years down the track I purchased another Ford Transit, but this time a half-decent one. This one was far classier, and in no time at all it was boarded out on the inside, with a partition across the middle. This meant a nice space at the back for the gear, and a separate section in the middle accessible by a side door, with a bench for three people and copious amounts of thick blue carpet everywhere for added style and comfort. This was in fact a brilliant van, that sadly never got to do as much touring as it deserved. Two people could sleep in it in reasonable comfort – well, two people who shared a certain level of intimacy anyway. It got me into trouble with the job centre though, who objected to me parking outside and walking in to sign on for my dole cheque, but I convinced them that it was a gift and that I certainly wasn't using it every week to do deliveries around the south of England as a part-time self-employed courier, no sir. It was in fact such a good quality van that for a while I was able to hire the van and my driving services to a friend's band. In a wonderful illustration of just how poor and unbusinesslike most bands are, the friends eventually decided that paying me fifteen quid to drive them into London and back for shows made no economic sense at all. After all, they could get their own shittier van which they could then drive themselves into London with, costing only ten quid in petrol money, thus saving five quid every gig. It wasn't a well thought out plan to be honest, as their old Sherpa van was a horrendous piece of crap, but fair's fair - after all, five quid is five quid.

Eventually I sold the van. I was twenty-two and sadly destined to never own a band van quite as cool as this one ever again. I down-graded step by step though, and got myself a little Vauxhall Astra van, which could fit all the band gear inside but could only carry two people. Now, you can put up with a lot of negatives in a vehicle, but having a rear door that shuts on only an intermittent basis is not really ideal. We discovered this when making our way home from a show, my drummer Trevor and I noticing that there seemed to be quite a lot of background noise to be heard as we cruised down the A41. On closer inspection this was due to the rear door opening itself and depositing one drum kit on the road some miles back – the drums, in their individual flight-cases, scattered at random intervals over the last couple of miles just outside High Wycombe, and the cymbals never to be seen again. For some reason Trevor took scant consolation from my informing him that oh well, the cymbals were shit anyway.

So for the next twenty years or so, much of my touring was done using either a rented van or the good old-fashioned car. The car has certain advantages, it has to be said. The fuel consumption is much better, the stereo facilities superior and the comfort levels generally a step-up. Unfortunately you generally need two cars, sometimes three, to do the job of the van, so any fuel savings are wiped out pretty damn quickly. And there are several distinct disadvantages too. For a start, anyone and everyone can see all the expensive and highly steal-able gear sitting in the car, so you can't leave the damn thing anywhere, at any time - even outside your own house once you get home in the middle of the night. I have immense sympathy for any musicians who suffer from their beloved gear being stolen – it's happened to all of us at some point - but so many times this happens because people have got home at 2am and thought sod it, I'll unload in the morning. Sure, unloading at 2am is shit, especially when you're in a second floor flat and you've got the damn bass amp in your car too, but it absolutely has to be done. Another problem is the company one must sometimes keep in sharing a car. The all-for-one-and-one-for-all attitude of travelling together as a band in a van is great, but sharing a car with just one other person for an eight-hour journey can leave one feeling suicidal if you draw the short straw. And then there's the risk of hangers-on undertaking the journey with you. I had a musician in the band whose husband accompanied her to just about every show we ever did. Not in itself a problem, as he would insist on paying for the fuel himself and that's the sort of currency a band can really get onboard with. In fact, there should really be nothing to complain about here at all. But writing this book is basically the nearest I'm going to get to therapy, so complain I will. To paraphrase Homer Simpson, I've seen plays that were more interesting that this guy. Plays! Coupled with this was an unwavering faith in the reliability of his satnav machine. This would regularly be deemed more trustworthy than my own directions, and would always end the same way – turning his Volvo around on a dirt track in the middle of nowhere in country Australia.

ACCOMMODATION

Having your loyal road crew drive you back to a nice hotel after a show - where one can wash the sweat off in the shower, change into a nice clean set of clothes, and perhaps enjoy a bite to eat with a well-earned relaxing ale at the quiet hotel bar, before getting a refreshing kip in a comfortable bed with clean sheets – is something I know for a fact that happens to some musicians, the lucky gits. As you will have already guessed, it's never happened to most bands, and certainly none of mine. Post-gig sleeping arrangements for myself tend to fall into any number of categories, some of which are just fine, and some of which you wouldn't wish on your worst enemy.

A very common thing for a band to do is a one-off gig. When you're free from the trappings of success, you needn't worry about the stress of doing a well-organised tour, say twenty-three dates around the country over a month, meticulously planned to minimise travel between shows and with a nice tour bus to sleep in or hotel rooms safely booked in advance. Instead you can enjoy the freedom of booking a one-off show in a town two hours from your home. Not quite far enough away that it merits splashing out on some accommodation - you're not earning enough anyway and besides, three of the band have to be at work by 8am the next morning. In fairness, the adrenalin that your body has worked up during the performance is a handy aid for keeping you totally wired for a couple of hours post-show, so at least falling asleep on the road is less of a concern, and if you are feeling tired then that's what caffeine was invented for anyway. Getting home to your own bed after a gig is a lovely thing in many ways, although it does lack a certain on-the-road charm[142]. But it's especially nice on a Friday or Saturday show, when you can sleep in the following morning before getting up and having all the requisite shower and breakfast facilities there at your fingertips. This works less effectively once you have kids, whereby you get home at 3am and get woken at 7am because the children really aren't onboard with the whole lie-in thing, and your partner is frankly less than enamoured at yet another few hours of solo parenting.

Sleeping in your car is potentially an option, certainly in countries with a climate like Australia, not so much in less furnace-like nations. But it ranks only one step above sleeping in a ditch really. While the car is sheltered from the elements, the ditch is almost certainly comfier and more spacious. Sleeping in a van is a step up

---

142 Note to wife – not in my case of course, I'm just saying it might. For some people.

from both, although far from ideal – for a start, the van is usually full of gear and distinctly empty of bedding. Nobody in their right mind wants to sleep across the front seats with a handbrake or gear stick in their back either. That said, the van came up trumps on one occasion I recall. We'd borrowed a rundown little Toyota van for a weekend of shows in Adelaide, a mere nine-hour drive away. As there were three seats but four people, someone was going to have to ride in the back with the gear. So a space was created with all the cunning of experienced musical equipment packers to enable the fourth person a nice cosy little nest of cushions in which to safely[143] recline. Despite being promised a couple of small rooms at the local YMCA, it turned out that it was in fact one large filthy dormitory to share with a gang of crusty old bikers. Upon realising this, I announced that someone should probably stay with the van, what with all the valuable gear that was inside it, and – in an act of heroic self-sacrifice – that someone would be me. Deciding that the YMCA car park wasn't the nicest spot to sleep in, I realised that the beach was only fifteen minutes away, so off I drove. I found a nice quiet spot, had a relaxing spliff or two and listened to the sea while I drifted off in my snug little nest in amongst the amps and drums. After a wonderful nights' sleep I woke refreshed, took a lovely morning dip in the ocean and headed back to meet the others for breakfast, pausing enroute only to nip into the conveniently located international airport for a nice hot shower. My comrades had unfortunately had a horrendous mostly sleep-free night, stuck as they were amidst a bunch of blokes apparently rehearsing for the World Snoring Championships. We did have another night to spend in Adelaide, but the rest of the band were adamant they were not staying the night there again, and no other suitable[144] accommodation could be found. This scuppered my plans

---

143 To a certain value of "safely".
144 Free or very very cheap.

completely, a shame, as I was rather looking forward to another night by the beach. Instead I was outvoted 3-1 on the motion of should we perhaps just drive home straight after the gig. After all, with four of us to share the driving this should be easy enough. This started off well with an enormous storm breaking as we left, and following us for the next two hours, making driving conditions a) bloody difficult and b) bloody exhausting. Post-gig adrenalin and a regular change of pilot meant the first half of the journey was just about bearable, but as the miles and the hours wore on I was so tired that I started to hallucinate at the wheel, which is never a good sign.

Sleeping in a vehicle is not always quite so pleasant. We did a show in Bournemouth in the deep dark depths of English winter. Some of the band were driving home afterwards, but Den and I decided we'd have a night out on the town after the show. In a supremely misjudged act of optimism, we didn't bother finding a Bed & Breakfast or a hotel in advance, as we figured we'd find a party to hang out at, or more likely some nice young ladies that would be only too happy to put us up for the night. So to speak. The problems with trying to have a big night out in Bournemouth were two-fold: firstly, it transpired that the town had a curfew, so all the pubs and clubs had to be closed by 1am. Secondly, by the time we'd left the venue of our gig, the only place open was a very dodgy nightclub that we'd never have remotely considered going into under normal circumstances. But desperate times call for desperate measures – it was cold, we needed beer, we had no choice. Unfortunately two young men in silk shirts, eyeliner and nail polish categorically do not blend in in nineties Bournemouth, and after getting some beers in we were slowly surrounded by a bunch of drunken meatheads, in regulation drunken meathead uniform. They were absolutely not going to put up with the likes of us in their territory, and after quickly exhausting their supply of verbal abuse, which centred mostly around the fact that I had both of my ears pierced, they decided it was time to up the ante. Identifying Den as the weaker of the prey, the decided they would set fire to him. Or rather attempt to set fire to him. This was a critical error on their part. Had they attempted to set fire to me, my fake "fur" coat would have gone up in flames in no time. Den, however, was wearing a coat that he'd picked up with remarkable foresight earlier that week from a charity shop – a former fireman's jacket! Try as they might, the dickheads simply could not get the coat to set alight, and as the bouncers came to investigate the trouble we legged it. Which left us out on the streets in the middle of the freezing night, alcohol-free and fuelled up on ecstasy with absolutely nowhere to go, hotels all closed and certainly no nice young ladies to be seen. As we fruitlessly searched for a safe haven we ended up on the pier, hiding out on a bench overlooking the sea and trying to roll joints and cigarettes with frozen fingers in the arctic wind. We gave up in the end, and made our way back to the car, where we sat shivering and watching little stalactites forming on the inside of the roof as the condensation from our breath froze. We never went back to Bournemouth.

Another option available that again is pretty viable in a nice warm country e.g. not Britain for most of the year, is the good old tent. I've played numerous festivals that offer free camping grounds to performers. Mostly this means a field that is more usually a football/cricket pitch, which is actually dead handy as the grass is short and the floor flat – something that can rarely be said about actual real campsites. You can then share the toiletry facilities at the clubhouse too, although this means the smell of Deep Heat and damp grass pervades the air at all times and there is never anything other than that weird tracing paper style of bog roll[145]. Early on I learnt that a roll or two of proper toilet roll should always be near the top of the key things to bring on tour, right up there with gaffer tape (duh), a torch, band aids, spare rizlas and back up tent pegs. Vehicular space considerations meant that any camping gear beyond a tent and bedding would be sacrificed before departure, but generally I rather enjoyed these trips. Before I ruined a perfectly good thumb betwixt two tent poles while erecting a palatial family-sized tent – scaring me off tents for good (see chapter 11) - I had a little one-man tent that took seconds to erect, and once filled with pillow, duvet and sleeping bag was something one could genuinely look forward to returning to, post gig. A quick aside - now, I'm no veteran camping enthusiast by any stretch, but I feel if I have one piece of advice to offer anyone else in this situation it would be never, ever, bloody ever buy one of those godforsaken fucking airbeds. They are always shit. They were *made* shit. Despite many attempts I have never spent a night on one that hasn't become a no-airbed by morning – and usually well before morning. Neither have any of my band mates. I have seen countless deflated airbeds stuffed into festival bins by musicians who have decided that, on balance, sleeping directly on the floor of the tent is infinitely preferable to sleeping on something that was specifically designed to be slept on and even has the word bed in its name. They all turn up for the next camping trip with a small roll of foam instead, which has the added benefit of not needing to be pumped up in any way[146]. But I digress. My tent was a lovely little escape pod from the

---

145 What bastard EVER decided it was fair to release that product into the market? I'd hate to have his karma in the next life (and I absolutely guarantee that it's a he).

146 This is in fact the most galling thing about the airbed, the fact that you exerted so much energy putting all the damn air in there in the first place.

madness of the festivals, and I've spent many a happy night gently drunk post-gig, enjoying a joint in the cosy confines of my little canvas dome, listening to the sounds of people swearing as they fall over tent guy ropes in the dark. Some people will of course complain about the noise of drunken musicians playing late into the night, but this was rarely a problem for me as I'd usually be one of those drunken musicians playing late into the night.

Of course tents aren't always magical little portals of comfortable solitude. I'm reminded of the festival in Canberra where some wag thought it would be a good idea to leave the 4000 megawatt floodlight that was next to the performers tents on for the whole night, forcing me into going to bed with sunglasses on. Or perhaps the night I was woken up by my tent poles punching me repeatedly in the face as they were bent in and out of shape by a ferocious wind – due to me being in it, it didn't blow away, but it was alas a write off the next day. A particular favourite was waking up at daybreak to the hideous call of an animal as it bustled around the door of my tent. The spinechilling sound was a frankly bloody terrifying portent of imminent death, and it was a good while before I plucked up the courage to take a peak outside, expecting to see some horrendous beast straight out the pages of an HP Lovecraft story, only to see that it was in fact... a peacock. Man, have you ever heard a peacock? They may not look scary, but by crikey they sound it.

Another option that festivals will often offer to performers is billeting, i.e. being given a bed by a local resident who has kindly volunteered their home to an unknown musician – commendable, but possibly foolish on their part I feel. I have never gone for this option myself. My instinctive dislike of all humans that I don't know (and in most cases those I do know), coupled with a desire for solitude and a complete disregard for the concept of a curfew precludes me from doing so. I have several band members who have tried the approach, and while I don't think it was ever quite the horror it could feasibly be, I note that none of them ever did it more than once and all of them stayed out as late as possible every night as it was "all a bit weird". Let's face it, musicians are usually on some level a bit weird too, and people offering their homes to unknown musicians are probably not completely normal, so it's not a combination that offers much hope. It's bad enough having to take a morning dump on a campsite toilet, the thought of doing it in a stranger's house is unthinkable.

Sometimes though, the festivals can really come through with goods when it comes to accommodation. We played one that gave us our own holiday house up in the hills and away from the festival, a beautiful spot with views to die for and all the modern facilities one could ask for. Another time we got a motel with a pool. A pool! Yeah! But these occasions were sadly rare. One time we got given keys to an enormous old house to stay in, but by the time we got there it was pitch black. We spent over an hour trying to work out how to get in, as there were four doors as far as we could tell, and we had a key ring with about fifty keys on it. Getting in your own house in the dark with your own key is challenging enough. It turned out the door we needed was hidden behind an older door that was unhinged and just leaning against the wall of the house, not exactly the easiest puzzle to solve in the dark. Still the house was ok once we got in, but there was no bedding. Fear not, there's a note here regarding the bedding! *"Your bedding is in a box on the porch of 45 Hidden Street, please collect it as soon as possible"*. This meant driving around a strange town late at night and entering people's property in an attempt to find a box to walk off with, so it was perhaps no wonder that the cops pulled us up to ask what we thought we were doing. We were entirely innocent[147], but I can happily concede that it certainly looked dodgy as all hell.

Variety is of course the spice of life, and variety is what you get when you explore the delights of staying at onsite accommodation provided by venues. It would seem churlish to moan about accommodation provided for free, and let's face it, if you're off the streets and indoors it can't be too bad, but fucking hell I've spent the night in some horrendous venues. Even factoring in the high chance that you'll be exhausted and probably slightly drunk and/or stoned on these occasions, capable of sleeping wherever you drop, sometimes you can't help but think that under normal circumstances you would only be approaching this room with a flamethrower. I recall a room above one great little venue that we were delighted to find out was available to us for free. We've already well established that I have a misguided inclination to doubt the truth of the axiom that you get what you pay for, so I was hopeful that free could mean actually really rather nice all things considered. It wasn't, of course. Three bunks crammed into a little room is absolutely fine, but three bunks fitted with mattresses made entirely of stains and bedding that hasn't been washed since the pub opened several decades prior and that you have no option but to use is something that no amount of alcohol makes

---

[147] Well... innocent of any of the things that the cops were suspicious about anyway.

you completely comfortable with. I had a terrifying nightmare that I was being repeatedly bitten by a spider and my arm was swelling up like a balloon, before waking in the morning to find that I had been bitten repeatedly by a spider and my arm was swelling up like a balloon. A hospital visit was probably required, but that was going to play havoc with the tour schedule, so we decided on balance that, as I was still alive, a hospital visit could be put off until I seemed like I might die or at least pass out. As it transpired, I *did* pass out, but then came back to consciousness feeling much better and markedly less swollen before a hospital was found[148], so it all worked out fine.

One of the quirks of Australia is that every pub was, or is, actually not a pub but a hotel. This is because of legislation that was enforced until the late 1980s, which stated that you needed to provide accommodation to get a licence to serve alcohol. While the cities may have plenty of modern bars, outside of that the venues are old hotels. This means that rooms are available - and they are *always* available, because the last time any work was done on them was indeed in the late 1980s, and even the worst hotel proprietor thinks twice about actually advertising them as accommodation for humans to pay for. Again, the venue is only too happy to offer you the room for free, and again you think well that's a right result, and again you find that oh dear God what have I done? I once stayed in a filthy room complete with a sink in the corner which was overflowing with a black liquid of unidentified component elements. I tried to swap rooms with the keyboard player Tom, who readily agreed, which I should have seen as a warning sign. On swapping rooms I discovered that his

---

148 Allegedly they were looking for a hospital. I'm far from convinced that this was the case, but I can't prove anything.

had the same sink issue, with the added bonus of blood on the walls and the bed frame. At some point someone at the "hotel" will have suggested that cleaning the rooms up is perhaps worth considering, and presumably the owner has said nah, don't bother, we don't use the rooms now unless a band wants to stay the night, and I'm not cleaning up blood just for a musician. There was one venue we visited a few times that in its day[149] would have been a pretty slick establishment. We would ascend a grand staircase up to any number of rooms that were available to choose from, with fresh(ish) bedding to boot, and some of the rooms didn't even have bed bugs. There was a balcony that linked all the rooms, and we'd end the night sat out on it above the main (well, only) road through the town, smoking joints and keeping an eye out for the rumoured ghost truck that supposedly drove through the town each night, always hugely disappointed when it failed to show up. The downside was the balcony was actually quite high up, and the wood, well, less than solid. Still, there were a couple of traffic cones marking the weak spots, so as long you stayed away from them you could be at least fifty percent sure that you were safe. By the time we'd make it to the balcony though, we'd have drunk our fill of free beer that was happily served up by the owner until he could stay conscious no more. Stumbling around pissed and rotten balconies doth not maketh good companions however, and one drummer was very lucky that when the floor gave way the hole that opened up was only big enough to accept his legs, leaving him free to dangle helplessly while the rest of us took pictures and laughed at him, before finally rescuing him and realising that maybe now would be a good time to not sit out on the balcony anymore.

---

149 June 2nd, 1930.

It's been known on occasion for a fan to offer their homes as a place for the band to stay. If you still have nowhere to stay by the time you hit the stage then be sure to casually drop into your between-song-banter that you need somewhere to sleep that night. This happened a few times when I was younger, and playing to younger crowds that were still stupid enough to volunteer their services, but it doesn't happen anymore. I have no problem with this, as the last time it happened we went to a fan's home and they sat us down in the lounge, brought in some beers and put some hardcore porn on the TV. What sort of person does this?! I slept warily and lightly that night. Still it could be worse. We once stayed with a bloke we met at a show who lived "nearby", nearby being a half hour drive out into the middle of nowhere. Well, it's better than a ditch, presumably. No actually, it turns out that that's not always a safe presumption to make. After our host polished off eighteen of our twenty-four beers within half an hour and passed out in the kitchen, I went and slept on the floor of the "lounge"[150], on a carpet which was made entirely of very old dirt. Even the dirt was dirty. I woke throughout the night, the rats under the floor keeping me from getting much sleep, and got bitten half to death by whatever the hell sort of bitey thing was able to live in that carpet. Early in the morning I met one of my companions on the way to the toilet, and we decided that a quick and quiet escape before our host woke was the way to go. Remarkably, I seemed to have had a more pleasant night than the others, one of whom refused to talk about it, ever.

Staying at another musicians' house, for example someone that you've shared the bill with, is always a win in my experience. Musicians

---

[150] Technically. In reality it was more of a scrapyard of old motorcycle parts.

understand each other for the most part perfectly, and know that all you really want is a nice cup of tea, an hour or two to chat and maybe listen to some tunes while the adrenalin wears off, and a clean sofa or floor. I'm sure other people may have horror stories of this sort of scenario, but I can only say that I don't and I'm grateful to all the awesome comrades that have provided a place to lay my head over the years. Although now that I write this, I'm wishing there could have been at least one weird nutter. But alas no.

SEX AND DRUGS

If you were in a famous rock band like Led Zeppelin in the seventies, or perhaps a glam metal band like Motley Crue in the eighties, it seems that you were obliged to spend the vast majority of your time taking drugs or having sex, or both at the same time. I'm not convinced the same lifestyle exists at the lower end of the scale. For a start you lack the requisite fame and/or money that is so important in attracting the opposite sex. I mean let's face it, most musicians need all the help they can get – nobody was shagging Guns'n'Roses for their good looks. Similarly, it's very hard to have a serious drug habit if you're in a band, as you simply can't afford it. Not a good habit anyway. I think this is one of the reasons the likes of Keith Richards or Ozzy Osborne managed to live through their years of excess – they could afford the good stuff. If they'd been buying all that heroin on street corners from dodgy geezers covered in scabs they'd have been dead in no time, but getting a better class of drug surely makes the habit a more viable long-term proposition.

Despite the romance of the junkie musician, and the seemingly intrinsic link of drugs and music, actually creating anything while seriously off your face is nigh on impossible anyway. Many times people have talked up the likes of The Beatles and Pink Floyd recording classic works while under the influence of acid for example, but nobody records anything good under the influence of acid. Try it if you don't believe me. If you can pick up your instrument and play *anything* after taking an LSD trip, then you've purchased some shit acid and should find a new dealer. Ditto heroin and, well, anything hallucinogenic. It's like trying to play cricket after fifteen pints of ale, or going skiing after a bottle of tequila, only much worse.

As you'll have gathered if you've made it this far through the book, I have had a fondness for marijuana throughout my life and, although I no longer smoke it, I still enjoy it every now and then in its edible form. It's a very long time now since I've taken anything harder than that. By my mid-twenties I'd realised that hard drugs and playing music don't really mix, at least not at the same time. For a brief period in the mid-nineties my band at the time did a run of gigs driven by amphetamines, the main effect of which was that you got through the set really really quickly. Then the next band I played in was not adverse to a little cocaine or ecstasy to help things along, but this came to a head at a gig that went disastrously wrong. I had rather misjudged my ecstasy intake[151] – for a while the gig was brilliant and I was having a fine old time, but towards the end I realised I may have overdone things somewhat, and spent the last few songs playing guitar while resting my head on the shoulder of Robbie the singer, so as to stay upright. This worked for a couple of songs, but Robbie

---

151 By taking some, instead of not taking some.

was similarly afflicted and in the end we both stumbled over into the stack of PA speakers, which collapsed over spectacularly, one of the speakers bouncing down a set of stairs and smashing a window in the process and, well, there was no encore[152]. My recollections of the rest of the night are hazy at best, but what I do know is that somebody poured cement down all the toilets that night[153], the police were suddenly everywhere, and the venue closed down later that week, never to open again. I know not whether we had any direct bearing on this. After this show, to our credit[154], we banned the consumption of any drugs until after the performance, although I applied for, and was given, a special dispensation to continue smoking pot.

One of the effects of smoking marijuana however is the paranoia it can bring on. By the time I was singing in a band again, I really struggled to function well if I was stoned, as singing in front of a crowd of people is not a good situation to be in if you're paranoid. So, to my credit once more[155], I banned myself from smoking a joint in a two-hour period prior to going on stage, which was really rather sensible and paid off accordingly. Still, I made up for it afterwards. I've never really coped well with the adrenalin which courses through your veins when you finish a gig, and for many years the first thing I would do post-show was find a quiet corner and light up. After ten minutes I'd be in a much better place and able to enjoy the rest of the night without feeling so manic. When I gave up smoking, the first few times I came off stage and didn't have a joint waiting for me were

---

152 Not because the crowd didn't want one though – they did, we were just physically incapable. Also we had smashed the speakers.

153 I have no idea why. And the fuck who goes to the pub with a bang of cement?

154 I'm aware I'm setting a fairly low bar for credit here.

155 See above.

positively frightening. I had no idea what to do with myself until I remembered I did rather enjoy beer.

Being a musician entails long periods of boredom, which is why drugs become more attractive. I always found weed to be an essential tool in the studio, either to help me get through listening to five hours of drum takes or to perk me up every now and then during a fifteen-hour mixing session. Despite its reputation with those who don't actually know what they're talking about, for the habitual user weed can perk you up just as well as caffeine for an hour or two (although for the occasional user it just fucks you up completely). Which works really well, up to a point. Once that point is reached – and there are a number of variables which make this point very hard to identify until you see it the rear-view mirror by which time it's too late – your brain basically throws up its hands and says right, I've had enough, no more. Then you simply have to call it a day.

Marijuana is also a handy tool on the road. Especially when you're on tour in Australia, and regularly driving distances well in excess of several hundred kilometres. I could never have coped without it, both in a physical sense (reducing the chronic back pain from hours sitting at the wheel or being crammed in the back seat with a bass player and a kick drum) and a mental sense (oh look, another road that goes in a straight line across a barren dusty landscape for two hours). And rolling a joint in a moving vehicle takes both time and concentration, so it relieves the boredom nicely. My sidekick Spider liked a smoke too, luckily, as it's a habit far more enjoyable with a little companionship. In later years I've had some younger people playing in my band, as well as finding my band playing with younger acts at festivals, and it seems to be a far less commonplace habit with their generation. It never ceased to amaze me that when I'd be sparking up a joint, my young cohorts would be instead be happy with a nice cup of herbal tea, or eating a piece of fruit or a bag of raw nuts. Seriously, healthy food. In a band! On the road! Rock'n'roll is not what it was[156].

Not that what it was was always a positive was. I once played with a drummer named Craig, who whilst being a great mate and a lot of fun, had a memory like a sieve and this only got worse the more alcohol and/or drugs he consumed. He would drive a small truck during the day, and if he couldn't finish work in time then he'd drive himself to the gig and meet us all there – usually about ten minutes before we were due to go on, thus putting the rest of us through minor nervous breakdowns on a reasonably regular basis. Strangely, for a drummer, he was also popular with the fairer sex, and it was not unusual for a lady to spend some time with Craig post-gig in the back of his truck. Not perhaps the most salubrious of settings for a romantic entanglement, but I fear I'm in no position to judge anyone on this matter. On one such occasion, after a hometown gig, Craig was enjoying some quality time with a woman in said truck, until his girlfriend arrived at the venue and got wind of the shenanigans that may or may not have been occurring, and started hammering on the back of the truck. Craig hid the girl and opened the truck, informing his actual girlfriend that he'd been too drunk and needed a lie down. He then locked the truck and accompanied his girlfriend back into the venue, with every intention of heading back to the truck shortly after to gain closure on the previous rendezvous. Craig

---

156 This is probably for the best.

being Craig, however, had another drink, topped off with some coke and weed and soon forgot about the woman in the truck, eventually walking home with his girlfriend. This of course left a woman locked in a truck in the middle of the night in a now-empty car park, only to be discovered and released later the next day when a surprised Craig belatedly returned. An understandably furious woman headed straight to the police upon gaining her freedom, leaving Craig to defend a not unreasonable charge of something that looked suspiciously like kidnapping.

Drugs, for all their obvious drawbacks, are generally a much more profitable line of business than being a musician, but the two occupations can and do mix, and not infrequently. I had a guitarist, Carl, that I was working with and we were struggling to finance a tour. Carl was known to sell the odd small quantity of elicit substances, and he said he could exponentially increase what little money we had in no time, if I was happy for him to invest it in some products of questionable[157] legality. We're not talking Scarface quantities here, but equally this was several levels greater than anything I'd come across before. But I saw no drawbacks in this plan aside from a possible jail sentence - and I figured Carl would probably be the one to cop that, so whatever. It's easy to find guitarists and we needed the money. We duly travelled to Tower Hamlets - one of London's classier suburbs[158] - on the train, where we were met by a shifty looking gentleman in a suit who was standing by the open door of a very fancy BMW. Jumping inside, we were driven to a nearby apartment, whereby our friendly dealer gave us a lump of hash and told us to

---

157 That's just an expression really. There was no questioning the legality whatsoever.

158 <cough>

wait there while he popped out to collect our order from wherever he had to collect our order from. He was gone for some hours, but it was a sizeable lump of hash and his wife made a nice cup of tea, so all was well. When he finally returned it was clear that some polite social interaction was required along with an in-depth sampling of the goods supplied. He was fascinated by the fact we were musicians, although it was clear that Carl may have ever-so-slightly exaggerated just how successful we were. Hell I didn't remember anything about the European tour we'd done with Blur that year, but Carl seemed to recall all the details, so I guess we must have done it. When we finally entered the zone of acceptability with regards to leaving politely, our host told us to hang on, as he had something for us. As I sat there wondering what on earth this could be, pretty much the last thing I expected was nearly two hundred vinyl records from the 1980s, but that is exactly what we got. Turning down this generous gift was not an option as there was no way in hell we were getting on the wrong side of this guy, so he dropped us back at the tube station and we headed back across London, each carrying about twenty kilos of vinyl and a bag of mixed substances with a street value of about six grand. And each somewhat shit-faced. Luckily that afternoon there was a terrorist bombing in central London, so as we entered Oxford Circus to change tube lines, we were suddenly confronted by the sight of police absolutely everywhere. Our paranoid state was now in overdrive, but we finally made it across the city and back to Carl's street in Wembley, ready to drop. Only to find that Carl's street was in fact closed off by the police, who were also pouring in and out of the house next door to his. Trying our best to look like we never had any intention of entering this street, we carried on walking, eventually ending up sitting in the nearby park for two hours as we wondered what the hell we were going to do. As darkness fell we plucked up the courage to gather our stacks of vinyl and attempt to get home. Mercifully, the police presence was reduced at this point to one squad car and we had no problems. Upon arrival, we discovered from Carl's house mate that somebody in the house next door had been murdered that afternoon. So all in all a rather unusual day. We did subsequently raise the money as planned, but I made the sensible decision that I would not be financing any further projects by this means. And despite carrying forty kilos of vinyl all the way across London, there was not a single damn record amongst them that I actually wanted to keep, which was distinctly bloody galling.

DIETARY REQUIREMENTS

Eating on the road can be a truly horrible, horrible thing, but it's important to note that there are different levels of horrible. Top – no wait, bottom – of the pile is eating in country Australia. It's bad for everyone, but particularly bad for a vegetarian such as myself. Once you leave behind the more cosmopolitan cities such as Melbourne, Adelaide or Sydney[159], you're really in trouble. On about ninety percent of occasions that I'd enter a roadside café or service station, one would have the following "vegetarian" options:

1. Chips

2. Toasted cheese sandwich (with non-vegetarian cheese)

3. Larger serve of chips

If one was really lucky, one might have the option of a pie, filled with unidentified alleged vegetables, or even the more cordon-bleu option

---

[159] I say "such as", but that's basically it.

of a spinach and ricotta roll. Usually though, the establishment will only order one vegetable pie to every six hundred beef pies, so you must be exceptionally lucky to sample one of these dubious delights. Once you reach a small town though, the world is your oyster. The local hotel will offer a wide range of culinary delights ranging from chicken parmigiana with chips, to chicken parmigiana with salad. Every small Australian town will have a chippy, and the more exotic adventurous places may even branch out into pizza – although some of course will have nothing to do with all that foreign muck. Talking of which, on some occasions you'd be lucky enough to find somewhere that not only sold all that foreign food, the place would even be run by foreigners too. The very nerve! Although I recall one Chinese restaurant in rural Victoria that had some local Australian waiting staff, and when we asked a few questions about the food on offer we were informed – very politely it must be said – that they *"weren't really sure about the food, all this Chinese stuff is a bit weird isn't it?"*.

And, as if it wasn't already tricky enough to find good food, as the start of the show edged closer I'd find myself far too keyed up to consider eating, and come the end of the show it'd be an hour or two later before I could manage food. At which point everywhere is closed anyway. I soon expanded my small list of essentials to take on tour to include a large box of assorted muesli bars, which duly saved me from starving to death on numerous long trips.

By contrast, touring in England was positively a feast of culinary delights. Despite the generally poor reputation of British food, for the touring musician the place is a bloody God-send. Even the most shambolic out of the way service stations all seem to stock a wide variety of fresh sandwiches, including numerous options for the non-flesh eater. Triple Ploughman's sandwich and a box of Jaffa Cakes? Don't mind if I do thank you very much.

Mind you, Australia is quite capable of coming through with the goods when it puts its mind to it. For years we'd do regular weekend lunchtime acoustic gigs at a hotel that, while offering a very average fee for a three to four hour set of tunes, would feed us a slap-up meal from the really rather good restaurant upon completion of our labours. Free beer all afternoon too, and that's actual real premium amber ale tap beer too, not a free can of VB[160]. Definitely one my all-time favourite venues.

You can eat very well at the decent sized festivals, due to the proliferation of assorted food trucks on site, but after gozleme for breakfast, falafel for lunch and a baked potato with seventeen toppings for dinner, you realise that it's perhaps slightly uneconomical to do this, and find yourself crying out for a cheap serve of chips to reduce your fiscal loss on the weekend. Although I once got to know a purveyor of some rather fine veggie burgers who frequented numerous festival sites, and struck a deal whereby we'd come and busk outside their stall for twenty minutes in return for free burgers.

---

160 VB (Victoria Bitter), for those who have not had the pleasure of a previous introduction, is one of the worst beers known to mankind. It is no coincidence that it is made at the same brewery in Melbourne that came up with Carlton and Crown, both equally horrendous and equally likely to be supplied to you for free by venues in and around the Melbourne area.

They got some music and some extra trade as a result, and we got fed for nothing. That's the way to do it!

But what about the rider I hear you ask? Yes, I have often asked this question myself. Last time I toured the UK at least half of the venues gave us a very decent pub meal for free, but this is not a situation that has happened on a regular basis down towards the bottom of the ladder. You get to specify basically nothing, be they refreshment requirements or technical stage requirements. You get what you're given. Actually being provided food before or after a show almost never happens. Liquid refreshment is more common, but certainly not a given. Some venues will give out a bunch of tickets to the band, and you can exchange them throughout the night for a beer – albeit usually the cheapest, crappiest beer, but beggars can't be choosers. I think I can count on one hand the number of times I've turned up to a venue and actually been shown a fridge or a table full of food and/or drinks. The opportunity to actually contractually specify a rider that includes a no-brown-M&Ms-clause has sadly never arisen.

13
THE ROYALTIES

I'd always rather naively presumed that royalties were paid to a musician by their record label. So if you were an independent artist with no label contract, you got no royalties - unless perhaps you were lucky enough to have one of your songs recorded by Madonna, in which case your pension was sorted. There was a vague notion that you could earn good money by getting your songs played on the radio, but nobody ever seemed to know how that worked, as it never really happened to anyone you knew. I mean it's not like they teach you these things in school. You don't get a leaflet with your first instrument explaining how all this stuff works. I had no idea that as long as you were a member of the relevant organisation, such as the PRS (the UK's Performing Rights Society) or APRA (Australian Performing Rights Association), you were entitled to payments for both mechanical and performance royalties – which said organisation would collect and distribute for you.

So what exactly *are* performance and mechanical royalties? Well, performance royalties are - believe it or not - royalties paid based on performance of your music. This covers any time your music is played on the radio or television. Except when it doesn't. Many smaller radio and tv stations are not monitored by the performing rights organisations, as I'm told it is deemed too much work for them to log every piece of music played and report accordingly (many, although far from all of them, being not-for-profit and run by volunteers). These of course are exactly the places that are most likely to play something that isn't part of the commercial mainstream. Of all the hundreds of times that my music has been played on radio and television, about nine of these times have been on commercial stations that have actually earned me a royalty payment. Thus those who do earn the royalty payments are more often than not the artists who are already established names. I received a royalty payment of about thirty dollars for one song being played on national radio in Australia. The mind boggles at the sums earned by, say, the latest Taylor Swift single as it gets its eighth play of the day on a commercial radio station, that has played it on rotation for the last month. Multiply that by the other fifteen stations in the country that have been playing it too, and then remember that there are another fifty countries doing the same and, well, you get the point. Imagine the royalties a song such as Queen's We Will Rock You has earned over forty-odd years of regular airplay, a song still getting played to death on classic rock radio all over the world on a daily basis. Anyway, as you can tell, these royalties are not a major income stream for those artists lacking in any form of commercial success, more an unexpected bonus that appears once in a blue moon and helps you buy a couple of new packs of guitar strings. Worry not, however, as there is more to performance royalties than just airplay.

Performance royalties also cover every time a song is played live. What this means is that every time you play one of your songs at a gig, you get paid for doing so. This is a discovery which I unfortunately didn't make until after I'd already performed about two hundred gigs[161]. I mean, this is a real bonus, I've already been paid for the gig[162], now I'm getting paid for it again, woo-hoo! In my busiest years I was earning several thousand dollars in live performance royalties, which is an enormous amount of money to the struggling musician.

To get these payments, you have to report annually to the relevant organisation the songs you have played and the venues that you have played them at. Unbelievably, despite patiently explaining this to several independent musician friends over the years, all of whom would routinely play a hundred or more shows a year, none of them could ever be bothered to report their live performances. I don't know if they just didn't believe me or were simply lazy, but you don't look a gift horse in the mouth in this industry. Venues must pay annual licence fees to have live music, and the PRS, APRA etc will then distribute this money to the artists that report their performances. Quite how this is worked out I'm not entirely sure, but I think the length of the song is a factor in how much money it earns. And obviously you'll only earn money for performing your own songs - but if you report that you played a bunch of cover versions then the writers of those songs will get paid accordingly. This is of course an open invitation to not report cover songs that you performed, and instead replace them in your annual report with your own songs – preferably ten-minute epics. I ~~know~~ imagine that these annual reports are ~~always~~ sometimes works of fiction, as most bands are crap at general administration, and keeping a copy of all your setlists

---

161 Bugger.
162 Well, sometimes anyway.

when you performed 87 shows that year is unlikely to happen. But an unfixable flaw in this process is that nobody can possibly audit the reporting musician anyway.

I've inadvertently stumbled upon another flaw in this reporting process too, and I suspect I'm far from the only one to do so. Part of being a member of the performing rights associations is registering your songs. I've got about 150 songs registered - basically the title, the length, the writers and the arrangers. For co-written songs, you assign a percentage of credit to each writer. When a song is reported on a live performance, a radio play or a television play, it is matched up with the relevant song title in the database, and the royalty payment assigned accordingly. The flaw of course is that many songs share titles. If reporting is incomplete, or perhaps the artist name is different to the actual writer's name, the royalty payment can be misattributed. I guess this is how it happens anyway. The important thing is that it happens. I know this because I have earned several thousand dollars in royalties for two songs that aren't mine. In one instance I had registered my band's arrangement of a traditional folk song – you don't get the writers credit obviously, as the song is in the public domain and free to use as you wish, but you do get an arrangement credit specific to your version. Two years later I received a flurry of royalties from another band's recording of the song – same basic traditional song, but nothing to do with my arrangement. In the other case, I registered a new song which to this day I am still yet to record, release or perform. However the title must have matched another song that was clearly getting a bit of airplay, and I inadvertently seem to have reaped the rewards. One wonders how many other times this happens, and how many songs have mistakenly earnt millions of dollars for people that had nothing to do with them. Come to think of it, I wonder if other people have inadvertently profited from my songs? I rather doubt it, but I will never know.

The other type of royalties are the mechanical royalties. These are royalties from the sale of physical products (i.e. vinyl, CDs etc) and from online services – streaming on services like Spotify, or digital sales on iTunes, Amazon et al. As an independent artist who has never been signed to a record label, the money from sales always came directly to me anyway, but I now get regular reliable payments from streaming (predominantly Spotify and YouTube). Reliable in two ways: firstly, the payments turn up on time like clockwork. Secondly, they are, without fail, reliably low. The lowest payment I received for a financial period was 3 cents. Funnily enough, checking my statement I could see that I'd actually earned 2.9 cents, but they'd had to round it up. At the time of writing, 2.9 cents equates to about 41 song streams on YouTube, or a mighty 7 streams on Spotify. It's slightly galling to work out that I need 5,000 streams on Spotify to earn the same money as I'd earn from one CD sale, but that seems a positively excellent deal when compared to the 28,000 streams I'd need from YouTube. I'm not going to bang on about the unfairness of these rates – if nothing else it would seem hypocritical of me to whine about it when I listen to so much music this way now myself – but I would point out that as of 2019 the owner of Spotify is now worth several billion dollars, more than double the worth of the two richest musicians of all time (reported to be Paul McCartney and Andrew Lloyd Webber). Which just about perfectly sums up this industry!

14
ENCORE

I am vaguely aware that this whole book might come across as an enormously lengthy and bitter whinge. It's not supposed to – putting my experiences into writing has reminded me just how much I've loved the journey, and how much fun I've had! I'm totally accepting of the fact that the likeliest scenario for my lack of tangible success in the music industry is in a large part due to my bands simply not being good enough, and I am completely fine with that. When I compare my work against that of my own musical heroes, I feel frighteningly inadequate. And as a producer friend of mine was fond of saying, the cream rises to the top. Although as another friend was fond of retorting, yeah but shit floats. I personally would like to add that most milk these days is homogenized, and the cream as a result is broken up into minute particles that will remain suspended within the milk rather than rising to the top. Also, I've produced many a turd that has been far too weighty to float.

Still, while any commercial success has steadfastly eluded me, I have had a wonderful time. Which isn't to say I don't have any regrets. Too many times I took a wrong turning, listened to other people instead of my own instincts, or behaved like a bit of a dick. Such is life. But

I always wanted to play in a band. It seemed like a damn cool way to live your life, and so it proved – although maybe for different reasons than I initially suspected. I've done it for thirty years and counting, and I feel a sense of genuine achievement about that, coupled with a vague notion that I have completely wasted the best years of my life. Sure, it would have been rather lovely to have had perhaps one hit song, just the briefest of taste of the rock star life. If only to know what it really felt like. But as I got older I realised that this wasn't why I was doing it anyway. In fact, the main things that perhaps the outsider thinks of as defining aspects of the rock'n'roll musician – glamour and riches, fame and decadence - turn out to be a complete irrelevance. The reason I, and so many others, continue to do this is to keep experiencing the magic of the creation and performance of music. And it *is* magic. And if you can keep doing this year after year, despite facing more rejection annually than most people face in a lifetime, then you have definitely succeeded on some level, even if not in a fiscal sense. What was also magic was that my journey led me to making unexpected friendships with of couple of my biggest musical heroes, both of whom turned out to be thoroughly lovely chaps, and every time I remember this it brings a smile to my face. One of these heroes was kind enough to enthusiastically tell me that one of my songs was "fucking ace" and you've got to be happy with that. *That* was cool. *That* was success.

Upon reflection, I think that, aside from the music, the main thing that makes being in a band such a rewarding experience is something to do with being in a gang. A belonging to an exclusive tribe, a family much greater than the sum of its parts. You might spend all day working in an accountancy firm, a real estate agency, or a shop, with the same four colleagues every day, but that doesn't feel like a gang. That's just a bunch of people you work with. But a band is a gang, and perhaps connects with some long-lost spirit of belonging to a tribe, that for most people remains buried deep and forever unseen in the DNA. Or maybe it simply reconnects you to your lost childhood, to the gang of mates you hung out with as a kid and all the little adventures that you went on. Everyone wants to go on adventures, and a band goes on them all the time. Except now you've got a shitty van and a bag of cables instead of bicycles and a bag of sweets.

If you're embarking on your own travels then I hope some of the advice contained in these pages proves to be of value. I do suspect that most of the crap I've been through on my own adventure is fairly unavoidable, part of the terrain that everyone must traverse if one is to go on the journey in the first place, but at least now you'll know it's coming. The journey doesn't really appear to have a destination either – the path simply peters out when you lose interest, or just keeps meandering onwards until you drop dead. There is no roadmap, no correct route to take, although there are definitely wrong turnings.

My own adventure is not over, and the road doesn't appear to have petered out quite yet. But the rubber on my tyres is wearing very thin in places. As I write this I'm pushing fifty years of age, and it's damn hard to find the physical energy to keep a band going as well as a job and a family. Yet the urge is still there, and old habits die hard. It might be a road to nowhere, but it definitely took me somewhere. It's a magical road and I feel incredibly lucky to have been able to travel it.

15
GLOSSARY

Here be an explanation of some of the terms found in this book that a non-musician may not be familiar with...

Amplifier (Amp) - A really heavy box that you plug your instrument into, although it's usually only bassists and guitarists that absolutely have to have one. Bass amps in particular are prone to weighing more than a small herd of elephants, so you'd think bass players would try and find ground floor flats to live in, but no, this is never the case.

Bassist - Person who plays the bass guitar. Or indeed the double bass. Or both. Hard to find in the wild, their rarity is due not to being hunted to near extinction, but due to a) the ease with which they can find decent employment in other bands and b) the fact that when it all comes down to it, nobody really wants to be a bass player. Playing bass is the equivalent of having to go in goal when you play football. But, much like the goalkeeper, you can't really play without them.

Booker - The person who books bands to play at the venue. In theory, the booker should be a highly organised and efficient individual, with excellent people skills. In practice, the booker is completely unorganised and inefficient, with almost no people skills.

Capo - An over-sized bulldog clip sort of device that you can put on the neck of your guitar to change the key that you're playing in. Infinitely preferable than the other option of relearning the song with a whole bunch of different and possibly very difficult chords, but if you rely on it too much and then forget to bring it the gig, well, you're royally fucked.

Codec – Nope, sorry, still no idea. I could google it, but then so could you.

Demo – In ye olden days, this would be a cassette (the demo tape) of a couple of songs that the band has hurriedly cobbled together on the cheap so as to have something to play to bookers in an attempt to secure a gig. Don't do what we once did and just supply a couple of songs by a cool underground band that you love and presume nobody else has heard off, as it turns out to be exceptionally embarrassing when the booker has also heard of them and now knows what a bunch of untrustworthy wankers you are.

Derek Trotter – Legendary cockney businessman and entrepreneur.

Door Bitch – generally a sour-faced moody individual who is charged with taking the admission money from punters as they come into the venue in return for stamping the punters hand with a comically inappropriate stamp that last saw fresh ink in the previous decade. Probably quite cheerful in everyday life - but as door bitch they are understandably pissed off that they're missing the gig, unable to get to the bar, and always trying to beg extra change off the band – who of course have none.

Drummer - Almost certainly deranged in some way, shape or form, drummers are usually a law unto themselves. They often come with severe alcohol problems, and are capable of filling a van with their own equipment alone, all of which is utterly indispensable and well mate you'd bloody better find a way of getting all those toms in the van or I'm not playing. Invariably infuriating, and utterly indispensable, a band is only ever as good as their drummer.

Engineer – In the recording studio, the engineer is the person doing most of the actual work. Setting up the microphones, cueing the band in, getting the musician's sound just right, politely explaining to the drummer that he's not quite nailing it yet after the forty-eighth take, pretending that they really like the band – there is very little the good engineer does not do in the studio. Recording with a great engineer is no guarantee of a decent result, but recording with a poor one is a cast-iron guarantee of a shit result.

Fiddler - See violinist.

Foldback (Monitors) - Those wedge-shaped things that you see at the front of the stage. They're basically poor-quality speakers that project the sound back towards the band so that they can hear what they're doing. Well that's the theory. What they're mostly used for is creating squealing feedback when a musician goes anywhere near them, or allowing the singer to hear nothing but lead guitar for the entire set.

George Best – Breathtakingly good footballer and sideburn-wearer who became a Manchester United legend in the 1960/70s and, unlike all his contemporaries, looked and acted more than cool enough to have been a member of a hip rock'n'roll band. He once famously said "I spent a lot of money on booze, birds and fast cars. The rest I just squandered" – I rest my case.

Guitarist - About as rare as a seagull outside a seaside chip shop, guitarists are the most likely to have an uncontainable ego and generally be a pain in the arse, despite being the easiest musician to replace in any given band. Their amplifiers have two settings – off, and too fucking loud man, and they generally display a complete lack of understanding that there are actually other musicians in the band who are just as important.

Keyboard Player - Usually the most technically proficient musician in a band, due to being forced into learning to read music from the age of six, they'll drive everyone insane by consistently whinging about not being able to hear themselves properly through the PA whilst steadfastly refusing to buy an amp because they don't really need one because they can just plug straight into the PA.

Manager – Person who thinks the best way to help your band is not to take all the crap jobs away from you so as you can concentrate on the music, but rather to take 10% of your earnings in return for offering unwanted amateur suggestions for your song writing – i.e. the only stuff you actually enjoy doing and are actually any good at.

Mixing Desk – you'll find one of these in every recording studio, and with most PA systems too. Some of them are gargantuan lumps of equipment, with several thousand dusty little knobs, hundreds of short and brightly coloured leads sticking in and out of them, and a bunch of faders. They're used to set the volume level and effects of each individual instrument and microphone that is plugged into them. They are also huge repositories of dust, food scraps, bits of tobacco and assorted narcotics, to such a degree that your average computer keyboard seems like a biosafety laboratory clean zone in comparison.

PA - Public Address system. At heart, they're an amplifier (the "head") and some speakers. For the really small shows, you only need one that you can plug a couple of microphones into for vocals. For larger shows, they look like they've been made by NASA and require rocket-scientist-level expertise to operate. But whether you're using one that cost you $20 at a car boot sale or $35,000 from a very fancy shop, they all have one thing in common – getting a decent sound for where you stand on stage will be a bloody nightmare.

Producer – At the top end of the scale, the producer is basically your project manager in the studio, working in conjunction with an engineer to help create the band's masterpiece. As well as technical direction, the producer will have creative input over things such as song arrangements, song choices, instrumentation etc. At the lower end of the scale, the producer is the person paying for the studio – in other words, the person who runs the band, because this person doesn't already have enough to worry about.

Roadie – See alcohol disposal unit.

Singer - Usually the best looking member of a band, and almost certainly the most fragrant, the singer should always be paid more than anyone else and be kept happy with a regular supply of pot and beer. This will allow them to carry on operating on the higher intellectual level that is their natural home, and to concentrate on what they do best – carrying everyone else in the band.

Soundman – Well dressed, polite, passionate about their work and great time-keepers are just four things that you absolutely cannot say about the soundman. But the soundman can make or break any gig, by being either excellent or crap at their job. Even the world's best bands can be made to sound bloody awful by a crap soundman, although they rest easy knowing that if they make the band sound shit, it's the band that will get the blame for it.

Teenage Mutant Ninja Turtles – Impossibly irritating cartoon characters that for some inexplicable reason were massively popular in the late 80s/early 90s, and whose merchandise turned up in all manner of unlikely locations including (but not limited to) one of my earliest rehearsal rooms. Absolutely not fit to lace the boots of the Penguins of Madagascar or Shaun the Sheep.

Violinist - See fiddler.

White Plastic Chair – Um... how did this get here?

16
ACKNOWLEDGEMENTS

A big thank you to my friends and family for their encouragement and feedback along the way, and for helping jog my memory of the past where it was found lacking! You know who you are.

A special thank you to Annie in New Zealand for pointing out my mistakes and making my English betterer.

And an especially enormous thank you to Mark in Geneva for his generosity with his time, for his patience, for his advice, and for his general willingness to indulge my stupidity throughout the process of writing this book. As you slide down the bannister of life, may the splinters never point in the wrong direction.

www.ingramcontent.com/pod-product-compliance
Lightning Source LLC
Chambersburg PA
CBHW072334300426
44109CB00042B/1435